Praise for
In All Things

"If you're looking for a resource that not only teaches but also trains, this is it. *In All Things* encourages us as participants to be active learners, mining the book of Philippians with time-honored tools. Melissa Kruger invites us into the text, helping us move from observation to interpretation to application and finally to devotional reflection based on what we have learned. I know firsthand the richness of this approach. I'm thrilled to recommend this study and pray she writes many more."

—JEN WILKIN, author of *None Like Him*

"Melissa Kruger helps readers put their heads down into Scripture to explore what is before and underneath and around the text, offering helpful insights along the way that deepen understanding. Then she invites readers to look intently into the reality of their own lives to apply the truths of the text in meaningful and life-changing ways. This is a solid study of a short book from a trusted source."

—NANCY GUTHRIE, author of Seeing Jesus in the
Old Testament Bible study series

"If you have read Melissa Kruger before, you will know that she has a passion for the study and right interpretation of God's Word and a gift for helping others study and understand it for themselves. She is also disarmingly honest, an excellent writer, and a superb storyteller. *In All Things* is a devotional study through Philippians that will guide you and your group through this important letter with its message of unshakeable joy. I warmly commend it to you."

—LIGON DUNCAN, chancellor and CEO of the Reformed
Theological Seminary

"Daily life—from the world news to our own personal difficulties—often seems uncertain and unsettling. Each of us faces circumstances beyond our control and situations we never anticipated. At such times, joy can be elusive. *In All Things* is a bright light shining through the fog. With warmth and biblical wisdom, Melissa Kruger guides readers on a nine-week journey through the book of Philippians, bringing us to rest in the ultimate source of unshakeable joy, Jesus."

—MEGAN HILL, writer, speaker, editorial board member
at *Christianity Today,* and author of *Praying Together*

"Thank you, Melissa, for another excellent Bible study. What a fantastic format to set a busy mum up to succeed in developing her own spiritual life as she faces the ever-pressing demands of nurturing all those in her care! This is great subject matter to study together to reshape every part of life with a gospel, missional perspective!"

—KRISTYN GETTY, wife, mother, hymn writer, and singer

"Is it true that we can find real and lasting joy? Where do we even begin to look? Melissa Kruger has done us a great service. *In All Things* helps us with our search for unshakeable joy. You won't have to look for long (she tells you on the second page!): it's Jesus. Christ-centered, theological, and relatable; I highly recommend this book!"

—TRILLIA NEWBELL, author of *Enjoy, God's Very Good Idea,* and *Fear and Faith*

"Who doesn't want more joy? I love how Melissa Kruger guides readers in the way of Jesus, the way of grace and peace, no matter where life may take us."

—COLLIN HANSEN, editorial director of the Gospel Coalition and coauthor of *A God-Sized Vision*

"With biblical knowledge and practical wisdom, Melissa brings refreshing insight to a familiar topic: joy. This study of Philippians skips feel-good platitudes and simple self-helps and wrestles thoroughly with the passages of Scripture through meaning, interpretation, application, and communion in each week's focal truth. This study is so needed; I'm anticipating the many lives changed by unshakeable joy through these pages."

—RUTH CHOU SIMONS, artist and best-selling author of *GraceLaced*

A STUDY OF PHILIPPIANS

IN
ALL
THINGS

A NINE-WEEK DEVOTIONAL BIBLE STUDY
ON UNSHAKEABLE JOY

MELISSA B. KRUGER

Author of *Walking with God in the Season of Motherhood*

MULTNOMAH

In All Things

All Scripture quotations, unless otherwise indicated, are from The Holy Bible, English Standard Version® (ESV®), copyright © 2001 by Crossway, a publishing ministry of Good News Publishers. Used by permission. All rights reserved. Scripture quotations marked (NIV) are taken from the Holy Bible, New International Version®, NIV®. Copyright © 1973, 1978, 1984 by Biblica Inc.® Used by permission. All rights reserved worldwide.

Italics in Scripture quotations reflect the author's added emphasis.

Trade Paperback ISBN 978-0-7352-9114-0
eBook ISBN 978-0-7352-9115-7

Copyright © 2018 by Melissa Kruger

Cover design by Kelly L. Howard; cover photography by william-montout

Published in the United States by Multnomah, an imprint of the Crown Publishing Group, a division of Penguin Random House LLC, New York.

MULTNOMAH® and its mountain colophon are registered trademarks of Penguin Random House LLC.

Library of Congress Cataloging-in-Publication Data
Names: Kruger, Melissa B., author.
Title: In all things : a nine-week devotional Bible study on unshakeable joy / Melissa B. Kruger.
Description: First Edition. | Colorado Springs : Multnomah, 2018. | Includes bibliographical references.
Identifiers: LCCN 2017045187 | ISBN 9780735291140 (pbk.) | ISBN 9780735291157 (electronic)
Subjects: LCSH: Bible. Philippians—Textbooks. | Joy—Religious aspects—Christianity—Biblical teaching.
Classification: LCC BS2705.6.J6 K78 2018 | DDC 227/.60071—dc23
LC record available at https://lccn.loc.gov/2017045187

Printed in the United States of America
2018

10 9 8 7 6 5 4 3 2

For Shanna.
You shine as a light in the world (Philippians 2:15).

and

For my children, Emma, John, and Kate.
May the God of hope fill you with all
joy and peace in believing (Romans 15:13).

Contents

Introduction

An Invitation to Joy

If I could grant you one wish, what would it be?

Many of us might choose the classic beauty pageant answer: world peace. Or perhaps we'd join the chorus with Jeremiah the Bullfrog's friend and sing, "Joy to the world, all the boys and girls." More than money, fame, or success, most of us are hoping for something greater, something grander—something that will last.

We want joy. We hope for peace. We long for contentment.

Money, fame, relationships, health, and success—these things we chase after—are really just means to an end. We're hoping money can buy us some peace or relationships will bring us joy. However, life doesn't always work as we think it should. Stuff piles up all around us and fails to satisfy. The closest relationships can bring the greatest turmoil. So often these longed-for good desires—joy, peace, contentment—seem just beyond our reach.

You may have picked up this book hopeful. You want joy, and you're looking for a road map to find it. You may have picked up this book weary. You've tried every game in town and wandered every path on a quest for something more, only to find yourself emptier than when you began.

Hopeful or weary, I'm glad you're here. I'm thankful we get to study together for the next nine weeks. I'll tell you from the get-go this isn't a self-help book explaining my top ten secret strategies to find joy. You and I both need something much greater than we can muster up on our own. We need something outside ourselves, something stronger, something secure. This thing we're searching for, this thing we're hoping to find? Well, it's not really a thing. It's a person.

Spoiler alert: it's Jesus.

I know that may sound simplistic. It's too easy, right? However, there's so much more to Jesus than we realize. He's the creator, sustainer, and source of every good thing, and in His presence is "fullness of joy" (Psalm 16:11). The more we know Jesus, the more we know joy, peace, and contentment. As we pull back the curtain and study the book of Philippians, we'll understand how knowing Him more makes such a difference.

You may be wondering, "Why the book of Philippians?" Well, that's a good question. I didn't start studying Philippians with the intention of writing a book, nor was I expecting to find peace, joy, and contentment. They found me. I was simply trying to help a friend.

Years ago, I was walking along the streets of Prague, Czech Republic, with my friend Shanna. Our main goal was shopping—we were on the hunt for a pair of perfectly fitting jeans. While that didn't happen (does it ever?), we did share some rather hilarious moments in the dressing rooms. Nothing bonds a friendship like laughing uncontrollably while trying to squeeze into jeans right next to each other.

As we roamed the streets, our conversation quickly shifted to our personal lives. Shanna lives in Prague with her husband, Phil, and their three children. They moved there ten years ago—far from family and friends—to plant a church and share their faith with others. Even though Prague has a rich Christian history, it's currently one of the most atheistic cities in Europe.

Shanna was hoping to gather on a regular basis with some women she'd met through her children's school to study the book of Philippians together. However, she couldn't find a study she thought would work for those in her group. Instead of a video study, she wanted something that would help each woman learn on her own *and* offer opportunities for group discussion. She casually looked over at me while we were getting in the car and asked, "Will you help me? Will you write some questions on the book of Philippians for me?"

I wasn't really sure what type of questions I might come up with, but I said yes. How could I not? She'd moved her entire family overseas to share Jesus with others. Surely I could spend some time writing up a few questions for her group of women.

Well, as it turned out, I couldn't just write *a few questions*. I wrote an entire study. And the more I studied, the more I came to love the book of Philippians. Her simple request is the reason you're holding this study in your hands today.

Philippians is an invitation to joy, written by an imprisoned apostle Paul to believers in the early church who were suffering from opposition. His continual refrain throughout the letter is "Rejoice!"

His joy was unshakeable. His peace was secure. His hope was abounding. Where did he find such depths of riches in the midst of such dire circumstances? From what source did he drink that filled him so fully? How did he learn the secret of contentment?

Can I learn it too?

All these questions lingered in my mind as I read Philippians time and again. The more I studied, the more I recognized how different Paul's joy was from the happiness I usually seek. Too often I set my heart on fool's gold and false treasure rather than on the riches found in Christ. Worldly items—the perfect home, a dream job, an amazing vacation, or financial security—may provide momentary happiness but repeatedly fail to satisfy. It's not wrong to enjoy any of these items; they're simply insufficient for lasting contentment. All too quickly, they lose their luster.

As we study together, my hope is that you and I will learn to recognize (and put aside) misguided and unsatisfying methods for finding contentment and instead seek the One who is the source of abiding joy.

God has faithfully given His Word to us as the means to know Him and transform us. Each week of this study, we will use a simple three-step method to ponder selected texts of Scripture, all of which are printed in the book for your convenience:

1. Observation: What does the text say?
2. Interpretation: What does the text mean?
3. Application: How does the text transform me?

All three of these steps are vital in our study of the Bible. Without proper observation, it's impossible to have correct interpretation or application. Without interpretation, our observation can become a fact hunt, useful only for trivia knowledge. Without application, we fail to make the connection between God's words and our own lives.

I've organized the study into four days of homework per week. Typically, Day 1 will focus on observing the text by reading it carefully. Days 2 and 3 will usually center on interpretation, and Day 4 will be spent applying what we've learned. I've also included a Day 5 Devotional that's best read after you've completed your notes for the week.

I encourage you to complete each week's study over the course of the week rather than in one sitting. For the Scriptures to speak, we need time to soak them in and ponder what the text is saying. Studying for twenty to thirty minutes a day will allow you time to think and meditate. Just as food tastes better when it marinates, the Scriptures satisfy us more as we savor and reflect on them.

So let's begin. My hope and prayer is that as we study this book, we will become women of abiding joy. As the English Puritan minister Samuel Ward said,

> Keep your faith, and it will keep your joy. It keeps you even without ebb and flow, turning ever upon the hinges of heavenly joys. . . . Is it not fitting for the righteous to rejoice? What is a Christian but one who is joyful? Does not the kingdom of heaven consist in joy? . . . Show me your faith by your joy. Use your faith, and have joy; increase your faith and increase your joy.[1]

In His joy,
Melissa Kruger

Week 1

We Need More Than a Spiritual Experience

Joy in Salvation

Acts 7–16

If ever the world needed the witness and testimony of Christian people it is at this present time. The world is unhappy, it is distracted and frightened, and what it needs is to see stars shining out of the heavens in the midst of the darkness, attracting the world by rebuking that darkness, and by giving it light, showing how it too can live that quality of life.

—Martyn Lloyd-Jones

DAY 1: OBSERVATION

What Does the Text Say?

For four very long years (it felt like an eternity at the time), my husband and I dated long distance. He was in seminary in California, and I was in college at the University of North Carolina. We lived about as far from each other as we could and still be in the same country.

Email was yet to be invented, and long-distance phone calls came at a steep price. So we wrote letters back and forth to each other. He saved every letter I wrote him, and I did the same. Currently, they're stored up in our attic, treasures of the early stages of our relationship.

Perhaps you, too, have a treasured collection of correspondence. The words of loved ones are important to us. We read them time and again, and we save them, keeping them as reminders of relationships that matter dearly.

When we read the New Testament, it's easy to forget that many of the books were letters. Of course the writers were inspired by God through the Holy Spirit, but these letters also are historical documents, exchanged between actual people in an actual time and place.

For that reason, in this first week of study, we're going to begin in the book of Acts, which reveals some key details about the life of Paul (the author of Philippians). We'll also meet a few early members of the Philippian church.

As we read the book of Philippians in the days to come, it will help to keep in mind that Paul was a real individual, writing to a real congregation. His words are rooted in a historical context and have been saved for two thousand years.

The letters my husband and I wrote to each other might survive a generation or two. I hope my grandchildren find them and enjoy reading the words we wrote as our relationship developed. However, I doubt they'll last much longer than that.

In contrast, Paul's words have been preserved all these years for you and me. These words are still relevant because, ultimately, they are written by a God who is eternally relevant. While historically the book of Philippians records a conversation between Paul and his beloved brothers and sisters in Philippi, all of God's Word is a letter between God and His people, as He reveals Himself throughout the ages.

What a gift! The God of all the universe speaks to you and me. He invites us to come and learn from Him. We have an amazing opportunity before us today and for the next nine weeks. We get to hear from the Lord through His messenger, the apostle Paul. I cannot wait to dig into these truths with you.

I encourage you to open your time in prayer, asking the Lord to speak to you as you read and to give you joy in this time with Him.

We'll begin today by looking at Paul's arrival on the biblical stage. Known initially by his Hebrew name, Saul, he first appears in the book of Acts just after Stephen, a man full of grace and power, preaches and testifies to the Jewish rulers about Jesus, a message that sparks their anger.

Read Acts 7:58–8:3.

> [58] Then they cast [Stephen] out of the city and stoned him. And the witnesses laid down their garments at the feet of a young man named Saul. [59] And as they were stoning Stephen, he called out, "Lord Jesus, receive my spirit." [60] And falling to his knees he cried out with a loud voice, "Lord, do not hold this sin against them." And when he had said this, he fell asleep.
>
> [8:1] And Saul approved of his execution.
>
> And there arose on that day a great persecution against the church in Jerusalem, and they were all scattered throughout the regions of Judea and Samaria, except the apostles. [2] Devout men buried Stephen and made great lamentation over him. [3] But Saul was ravaging the church, and entering house after house, he dragged off men and women and committed them to prison.

1. List two or three things you learn about Saul from this passage.

2. Thankfully, Saul's story doesn't end there. Read **Acts 9:1–9** and answer
   the questions that follow.

   ¹But Saul, still breathing threats and murder against the disciples of
   the Lord, went to the high priest ²and asked him for letters to the
   synagogues at Damascus, so that if he found any belonging to the Way,
   men or women, he might bring them bound to Jerusalem. ³Now as he
   went on his way, he approached Damascus, and suddenly a light from
   heaven shone around him. ⁴And falling to the ground, he heard a voice
   saying to him, "Saul, Saul, why are you persecuting me?" ⁵And he said,
   "Who are you, Lord?" And he said, "I am Jesus, whom you are persecuting. ⁶But rise and enter the city, and you will be told what you are to
   do." ⁷The men who were traveling with him stood speechless, hearing
   the voice but seeing no one. ⁸Saul rose from the ground, and although
   his eyes were opened, he saw nothing. So they led him by the hand and
   brought him into Damascus. ⁹And for three days he was without sight,
   and neither ate nor drank.

   a. Why was Saul going to Damascus?

   b. Who appeared to Saul along the way, and how did Saul respond?

   c. What happened to Saul afterward?

3. The story continues in **Acts 9:10–19.**

[10]Now there was a disciple at Damascus named Ananias. The Lord said to him in a vision, "Ananias." And he said, "Here I am, Lord." [11]And the Lord said to him, "Rise and go to the street called Straight, and at the house of Judas look for a man of Tarsus named Saul, for behold, he is praying, [12]and he has seen in a vision a man named Ananias come in and lay his hands on him so that he might regain his sight." [13]But Ananias answered, "Lord, I have heard from many about this man, how much evil he has done to your saints at Jerusalem. [14]And here he has authority from the chief priests to bind all who call on your name." [15]But the Lord said to him, "Go, for he is a chosen instrument of mine to carry my name before the Gentiles and kings and the children of Israel. [16]For I will show him how much he must suffer for the sake of my name." [17]So Ananias departed and entered the house. And laying his hands on him he said, "Brother Saul, the Lord Jesus who appeared to you on the road by which you came has sent me so that you may regain your sight and be filled with the Holy Spirit." [18]And immediately something like scales fell from his eyes, and he regained his sight. Then he rose and was baptized; [19]and taking food, he was strengthened.

a. Who was Ananias? How did he feel about visiting Saul?

b. What specific ministry did God plan for Saul (verse 15)?

c. How did Saul respond to Ananias's words?

4. Continue reading Saul's story in **Acts 9:19–30.**

[19]For some days he was with the disciples at Damascus. [20]And immediately he proclaimed Jesus in the synagogues, saying, "He is the Son of
God." [21]And all who heard him were amazed and said, "Is not this the
man who made havoc in Jerusalem of those who called upon this name?
And has he not come here for this purpose, to bring them bound before
the chief priests?" [22]But Saul increased all the more in strength, and
confounded the Jews who lived in Damascus by proving that Jesus was
the Christ.

[23]When many days had passed, the Jews plotted to kill him, [24]but
their plot became known to Saul. They were watching the gates day and
night in order to kill him, [25]but his disciples took him by night and let
him down through an opening in the wall, lowering him in a basket.

[26]And when he had come to Jerusalem, he attempted to join the
disciples. And they were all afraid of him, for they did not believe that he
was a disciple. [27]But Barnabas took him and brought him to the apostles
and declared to them how on the road he had seen the Lord, who spoke
to him, and how at Damascus he had preached boldly in the name of
Jesus. [28]So he went in and out among them at Jerusalem, preaching boldly
in the name of the Lord. [29]And he spoke and disputed against the Hellenists. But they were seeking to kill him. [30]And when the brothers learned
this, they brought him down to Caesarea and sent him off to Tarsus.

a. Once Saul believed in Jesus, what did he begin to do (verse 20)?

b. What challenges did he encounter (verses 23–25)?

c. How did many of the disciples feel about Saul?

d. Who brought him to the apostles?

e. How do you think Saul's past affected his ministry to others?

Notice the abrupt transformation in Saul's life. The persecutor had become the preacher—and then the persecuted. Only a divine meeting could produce such a metamorphosis in Saul. He changed from being an enemy of the church to being willing to suffer for it. He went from being devoted to destroying the church to risking his own life to build it. Meeting Jesus changed everything.

The turmoil that began with Stephen's message continued to affect followers of Jesus, as well as Saul's ministry.

5. Read **Acts 11:19–26** and answer the questions that follow.

[19]Now those who were scattered because of the persecution that arose over Stephen traveled as far as Phoenicia and Cyprus and Antioch,

speaking the word to no one except Jews. [20]But there were some of them, men of Cyprus and Cyrene, who on coming to Antioch spoke to the Hellenists also, preaching the Lord Jesus. [21]And the hand of the Lord was with them, and a great number who believed turned to the Lord. [22]The report of this came to the ears of the church in Jerusalem, and they sent Barnabas to Antioch. [23]When he came and saw the grace of God, he was glad, and he exhorted them all to remain faithful to the Lord with steadfast purpose, [24]for he was a good man, full of the Holy Spirit and of faith. And a great many people were added to the Lord. [25]So Barnabas went to Tarsus to look for Saul, [26]and when he had found him, he brought him to Antioch. For a whole year they met with the church and taught a great many people. And in Antioch the disciples were first called Christians.

a. What happened because of the scattering that occurred after Stephen's death?

b. Where was Barnabas sent? How long did he stay there? What significant thing happened there?

c. How does this passage demonstrate the truth of God's words to Ananias about Saul in Acts 9:15?

Saul's salvation is a miraculous story. Not only did God change his heart, but He also set him apart as an apostle, giving him the special calling of authority in the church and, later, the privilege of writing the very words of Scripture. God intervened and transformed this man's life in an amazing way, setting him on a course to share the good news of Jesus with those outside the Jewish faith, who knew him by his Greek name, Paul. God prepared a ministry for Paul and prepared Paul for the ministry.

While we are unlikely to experience a blinding light on the road to Damascus, each of us has a story of faith that's a miracle in its own way. Your story may be just as dramatic as Paul's, or you may have experienced a slow awakening to faith. God calls each of us to Himself in different ways. Whatever way He worked in your life, the good news is that the scales that once blinded you to faith fell from your spiritual eyes! God has prepared a ministry for you and has prepared you for a ministry to others.

Close your time today by thinking about how you came to faith. Write down how you learned of Jesus and the ways you've seen your faith grow throughout the years. What particular moments, if any, stand out to you? Take time to praise God for the people and ways He used to call you to Himself.

If you're not certain you believe in God or Christianity, write down your questions. Do you have doubts? Are you fearful or distrustful of religion? What keeps you from believing in Jesus? Take time to pray that God would meet you in your doubts and that Christ would become real to you.

DAY 2: OBSERVATION

What Does the Text Say?

Yesterday we observed the amazing transformation that happened in Paul's life after his encounter with Jesus. He went from persecutor to preacher to persecuted.

In the course of his life, Paul traveled around the Roman Empire bringing the good news of Christ. Paul spent the majority of his time preaching to Gentiles (non-Jewish people). Accompanied by various other disciples, he made a total of three missionary journeys.

Today we'll consider Paul's second missionary journey, which eventually took him to Macedonia, a region that included the cities of Philippi, Thessalonica, and Berea.

We'll begin our study in Acts 15 and 16 to gain helpful insights about the people Paul wrote to in his letter to the Philippians. We'll divide it into smaller sections so you can reflect as you read.

1. Read **Acts 15:36–16:5** and answer the questions that follow.

> ³⁶And after some days Paul said to Barnabas, "Let us return and visit the brothers in every city where we proclaimed the word of the Lord, and see how they are." ³⁷Now Barnabas wanted to take with them John called Mark. ³⁸But Paul thought best not to take with them one who had withdrawn from them in Pamphylia and had not gone with them to the work. ³⁹And there arose a sharp disagreement, so that they separated from each other. Barnabas took Mark with him and sailed away to Cyprus, ⁴⁰but Paul chose Silas and departed, having been commended by the brothers to the grace of the Lord. ⁴¹And he went through Syria and Cilicia, strengthening the churches.
>
> ¹⁶:¹Paul came also to Derbe and to Lystra. A disciple was there, named Timothy, the son of a Jewish woman who was a believer, but his father was a Greek. ²He was well spoken of by the brothers at Lystra and Iconium. ³Paul wanted Timothy to accompany him, and he took him and circumcised him because of the Jews who were in those places, for they all knew that his father was a Greek. ⁴As they went on their way through the cities, they delivered to them for observance the decisions that had been reached by the apostles and elders who were in Jerusalem. ⁵So the churches were strengthened in the faith, and they increased in numbers daily.

a. Who accompanied Paul on this particular missionary journey? Who
    was noticeably absent?

b. List the regions they traveled through. (If you have a map of Paul's
    second missionary journey in your Bible, you may find it helpful to
    take the time to locate these cities.)

c. What did they do in each of the cities they visited? What was the result
    (verses 4–5)?

After years of preaching and traveling together, Paul and Barnabas separated
over a disagreement about Mark, who had deserted them on an earlier journey. On
this missionary journey, Paul traveled with Silas, Timothy, and Luke. (Luke is the
author of Acts, an eyewitness to these events.) After various twists and turns, the
Holy Spirit guided them to Philippi.

2. Read Acts 16:9–10.

⁹And a vision appeared to Paul in the night: a man of Macedonia was
standing there, urging him and saying, "Come over to Macedonia and
help us." ¹⁰And when Paul had seen the vision, immediately we sought
to go on into Macedonia, concluding that God had called us to preach
the gospel to them.

a. Describe the vision Paul had.

b. How did Paul and his fellow travelers respond?

Paul and his companions had three significant encounters during their time in Philippi. Let's look at each situation and observe what happened.

3. First Encounter: read **Acts 16:11–15**.

[11]So, setting sail from Troas, we made a direct voyage to Samothrace, and the following day to Neapolis, [12]and from there to Philippi, which is a leading city of the district of Macedonia and a Roman colony. We remained in this city some days. [13]And on the Sabbath day we went outside the gate to the riverside, where we supposed there was a place of prayer, and we sat down and spoke to the women who had come together. [14]One who heard us was a woman named Lydia, from the city of Thyatira, a seller of purple goods, who was a worshiper of God. The Lord opened her heart to pay attention to what was said by Paul. [15]And after she was baptized, and her household as well, she urged us, saying, "If you have judged me to be faithful to the Lord, come to my house and stay." And she prevailed upon us.

a. What do you learn about the city of Philippi?

b. To whom did Paul and Timothy speak by the riverside?

c. List three things you learn about this person.

d. How does verse 14 describe what happened as she listened to Paul's message?

e. How did belief in the apostles' message translate into action for this woman? What two things did she do in verse 15?

4. Second Encounter: read **Acts 16:16–24.**

¹⁶As we were going to the place of prayer, we were met by a slave girl who had a spirit of divination and brought her owners much gain by fortune-telling. ¹⁷She followed Paul and us, crying out, "These men are servants of the Most High God, who proclaim to you the way of salvation." ¹⁸And this she kept doing for many days. Paul, having become greatly annoyed, turned and said to the spirit, "I command you in the name of Jesus Christ to come out of her." And it came out that very hour.

¹⁹But when her owners saw that their hope of gain was gone, they

seized Paul and Silas and dragged them into the marketplace before the rulers. [20]And when they had brought them to the magistrates, they said, "These men are Jews, and they are disturbing our city. [21]They advocate customs that are not lawful for us as Romans to accept or practice." [22]The crowd joined in attacking them, and the magistrates tore the garments off them and gave orders to beat them with rods. [23]And when they had inflicted many blows upon them, they threw them into prison, ordering the jailer to keep them safely. [24]Having received this order, he put them into the inner prison and fastened their feet in the stocks.

a. What did Paul do about the slave girl who followed them?

b. How did the slave girl's life change? Why were her owners angry with Paul (verse 19)?

c. List everything that happened to Paul and Silas in verses 22–24.

5. Third Encounter: read **Acts 16:25–34.**

[25]About midnight Paul and Silas were praying and singing hymns to God, and the prisoners were listening to them, [26]and suddenly there was a great earthquake, so that the foundations of the prison were shaken.

And immediately all the doors were opened, and everyone's bonds were unfastened. [27]When the jailer woke and saw that the prison doors were open, he drew his sword and was about to kill himself, supposing that the prisoners had escaped. [28]But Paul cried with a loud voice, "Do not harm yourself, for we are all here." [29]And the jailer called for lights and rushed in, and trembling with fear he fell down before Paul and Silas. [30]Then he brought them out and said, "Sirs, what must I do to be saved?" [31]And they said, "Believe in the Lord Jesus, and you will be saved, you and your household." [32]And they spoke the word of the Lord to him and to all who were in his house. [33]And he took them the same hour of the night and washed their wounds; and he was baptized at once, he and all his family. [34]Then he brought them up into his house and set food before them. And he rejoiced along with his entire household that he had believed in God.

a. How did Paul and Silas respond to their imprisonment? Who listened to them?

b. What happened to the prisoners as a result of the earthquake?

c. How did the jailer respond when he believed all the prisoners had escaped?

d. What did Paul say to relieve his fears? How did the jailer respond?

e. How did Paul answer his question, "Sirs, what must I do to be saved?"

f. What four actions did the jailer take once he believed the message?

6. We find the conclusion of Paul's visit to Philippi in **Acts 16:35–40.**

> [35]But when it was day, the magistrates sent the police, saying, "Let those men go." [36]And the jailer reported these words to Paul, saying, "The magistrates have sent to let you go. Therefore come out now and go in peace." [37]But Paul said to them, "They have beaten us publicly, uncondemned, men who are Roman citizens, and have thrown us into prison; and do they now throw us out secretly? No! Let them come themselves and take us out." [38]The police reported these words to the magistrates, and they were afraid when they heard that they were Roman citizens. [39]So they came and apologized to them. And they took them out and asked them to leave the city. [40]So they went out of the prison and visited Lydia. And when they had seen the brothers, they encouraged them and departed.

a. The next day, the magistrates released Paul and Silas. How did Paul respond?

b. Who did Paul and his companions visit on their way out of Philippi?

Paul met many people during his time in Philippi. They represented various nationalities and stations in society. Lydia was a businesswoman from Thyatira, wealthy enough to be able to invite Paul and his companions to her household. He also met a slave girl, devoid of personal rights and used for the monetary gain of her owners. In prison, he interacted with fellow prisoners, who listened to his songs in the night. Paul also conversed with a Roman guard, sharing the gospel with his entire household.

Notice the diversity of those with whom Paul engaged: men and women, rich and poor, religious and nonreligious, politically connected and enemies of the state. The good news of the gospel is for everyone. No one is so good that she doesn't need the gospel, and no one is so lost that the gospel can't find her.

Take some time today to think of those in your own life. Do you know someone who needs to hear the good news of the gospel? Pray for that person, that the Lord might open his or her heart to the message, just as He did with Lydia, and that the Lord will give you opportunities to share.

Close your time in prayer, praying with David,

> Restore to me the joy of your salvation,
>   and uphold me with a willing spirit. (Psalm 51:12)

DAY 3: INTERPRETATION

What Does the Text Mean?

Today, we'll revisit the passage from yesterday, seeking to understand more fully what the text means. While observation questions are usually pretty straightforward and the answers are found directly in the text, interpretation questions allow us more time to ponder and consider the meaning of what we're reading. If you find yourself unsure of how to answer certain questions, that's okay! Keep pondering and prayerfully meditating on those questions throughout the day.

And be encouraged: our correct interpretation of the Bible is not the result of our own intelligence or understanding but of the Holy Spirit's guidance. Begin your time with prayer, asking God to give you wisdom and insight as you read.

To begin, read **Acts 16:9–40** again. You can find these verses on pages 15–20 in yesterday's study or read them in your own Bible.

1. What type of help do you think the man in Paul's vision was speaking about in verse 9?

2. It says that Paul and his companions went to preach the gospel to the Philippians. What is meant by the term *the gospel*? See Romans 1:16–17; 3:23–24; and 6:23 for additional insight.

3. In this passage we see that both Lydia and the jailer were baptized immediately after they believed Paul's message about Jesus. What is baptism, and what purpose does it serve? Acts 2:38–39 and Romans 6:3–4 provide further understanding.

4. Read **James 2:14–17.**

¹⁴What good is it, my brothers, if someone says he has faith but does not have works? Can that faith save him? ¹⁵If a brother or sister is poorly clothed and lacking in daily food, ¹⁶and one of you says to them, "Go in peace, be warmed and filled," without giving them the things needed for the body, what good is that? ¹⁷So also faith by itself, if it does not have works, is dead.

a. After they were baptized, both Lydia and the jailer addressed the practical needs of Paul and his companions. Why do you think they did so?

b. How do their actions exemplify the teaching in this passage?

5. In Philippi, Lydia and the jailer believed the truth of Paul's message; however, many other people responded with anger. What is the reason behind the two starkly different responses? See Acts 16:14.

6. How did God use the suffering of Paul and Silas in jail to bring people to belief in Jesus? How many people had the opportunity to hear about Jesus because of their arrest?

Reread **Acts 16:34**.

> Then he brought them up into his house and set food before them.
> And he rejoiced along with his entire household that he had believed
> in God.

7. What explanation would you give for how belief in God leads to joy?

8. Why is it significant that Paul and his companions sat down with
   Lydia and her friends, as well as made sure to visit Lydia on their way
   out of town? What does it say about their attitudes regarding women?
   How would their attitudes compare with the cultural norm at the
   time? (See John 4:27 for more insight about cultural norms in the first
   century.)

In the Greco-Roman world, the term *gospel* was often used by the emperor
after a successful battle. He would send his envoy ahead of him, declaring the
"good news" of victory. It led to rejoicing and celebration for all under the emper-
or's reign.

When Paul shared the gospel of God with the people of Philippi, he spoke as
an envoy of a heavenly victory. This same good news has traveled two thousand
years to reach you and me today.

The sin that entrapped us, that bound us fast, has been overcome. The judgment you and I rightly deserved has been pardoned! Christ's death on the cross paid
the penalty of our sin, and His resurrection assures our victory. Just as He was given
a new body, so we will be given new bodies. As He now reigns at the Father's side,
so we will reign with Him.

We have much to celebrate. No matter what happens in our lives, if we're under the reign of Christ, victory is secured. We may face hardships, struggles, relational discord, physical illness, and other painful trials as we journey. But we will overcome in the end. All will be made right. One day we'll be home with our King, fully at rest and secure for eternity.

It's this good news that filled the Roman jailer with joy. He'd lived his life under Roman rule. Think about what that entailed—he was prepared to kill himself because of an earthquake (clearly, not his fault) that may have caused the escape of his prisoners. What a heavy burden to live under.

In one instant of belief, his allegiance transferred to a higher kingdom. He understood his newfound freedom, and he rejoiced.

Close your time today in prayer, celebrating the gospel and meditating on these truths. No matter what is happening in your life, no one can take away your salvation. Rejoice!

> Blessed be the God and Father of our Lord Jesus Christ! According to his great mercy, he has caused us to be born again to a living hope through the resurrection of Jesus Christ from the dead, to an inheritance that is imperishable, undefiled, and unfading, kept in heaven for you, who by God's power are being guarded through faith for a salvation ready to be revealed in the last time. (1 Peter 1:3–5)

DAY 4: APPLICATION

How Does the Text Transform Me?

When my children were in preschool, a few of us invited all the moms to an annual back-to-school brunch. It was a time of fellowship and getting to know one another, but our larger purpose was to invite new ladies to our Bible study. We hoped that by studying the Bible with other women, we might have the opportunity to share the gospel. Out of the hundreds of invitations we sent, usually only a handful of ladies joined us for the study.

One year, I found myself sitting beside someone new. I introduced myself, and she told me her name was Debbie. I noticed a cotton bandage taped to her arm, and I asked if she'd just come from the doctor's office. She calmly told me her shocking news: "Last week I was diagnosed with breast cancer." We discussed her prognosis, and then our conversation turned to why she had come to the group.

"Well, I'm hoping to have a spiritual experience."

Her words rang in my ears. Here was a woman looking for something more. She was intelligent, successful, married to a loving husband, and the mother of two wonderful children. But deep in her heart, she knew there was something more to this life, something more she was hoping to experience.

In many ways, I think Debbie was similar to Lydia. We're told that Lydia was a "worshiper of God," which probably means she was a Jewish proselyte, a convert to Judaism rather than one born into a Jewish family. She regularly came to the river to pray and talk through the Scriptures with the other women gathered there. While she was a successful businesswoman and ran her own household, she was looking for something more.

Perhaps you, too, are searching for something more. Today we'll continue to study the same passage, this time considering what it means for each of us as individuals. We've observed and interpreted, and today we'll seek to apply it to our own lives.

Read **Acts 16:9–40** (printed on pages 15–20) one more time. Let these words settle into your heart and ask the Lord to give you wisdom and insight in applying them to your own life today.

1. Have you ever had an experience like Lydia's, when you really felt that the Lord opened your heart to hear about Jesus? If so, describe the situation. How did that experience change you?

2. In verse 34 we're told the jailer rejoiced that he and his family believed in God. The NIV states it this way: "He was filled with joy because he had come to believe in God." In what ways does believing in God bring you joy today? List two or three specific truths about Jesus that encourage you, even in the midst of difficult circumstances.

3. Paul and his companions suffered greatly as they took the gospel to the Philippians. It is easy to believe that for our lives to be full of joy they must be free of suffering. However, Paul rejoiced through song while facing hardship. Describe a time of suffering or sorrow when you experienced an unexplainable joy in the Lord or a time when you observed that joy in someone else who was going through a difficult season.

4. How does singing help you rejoice in the Lord? Name a hymn or song that helps you worship God, and note one or two of your favorite lines.

5. When suffering comes because of our faith, we can have a variety of responses. We may grow fearful, angry, or anxious and seek to hide our faith from others. Or we may become increasingly faithful, joyful,

prayerful, and bold. How would you describe your most common reaction to suffering? In what specific ways would you like to be more like Paul and his companions?

6. Paul's suffering allowed him opportunities to share the reason for his hope with the other prisoners and with the jailer and his family. How has God used your suffering to encourage others?

7. In this passage we see that knowing God leads to immediate action. After Paul saw the vision, he immediately left to go to Philippi. After Lydia and the jailer became Christians, they were immediately baptized. They also both felt the need to care for and serve Paul and his companions.

    a. Have you been baptized? If not, what prevents you from doing so? If so, what does your baptism symbolize?

    b. In what ways has your faith compelled you to care for the needs of others?

c. Who is someone you can care for and serve with joy today?

d. Think of someone in your life who needs to hear the good news. Could you invite this person to a Bible study or church service or perhaps some other event where he or she could hear the gospel? What are some other ways you could share the good news of Jesus with this person?

8. As you think back to the passages we studied this week, what truths did you learn about God? How does understanding these truths change you?

I'd like to end our time today sharing an email Debbie wrote to me two years after our initial meeting. She faithfully came to our study every week, asked tons of questions, and sought to understand the Bible. After her initial good reports that the cancer was clear, it returned but this time in her brain. Here's her story of what happened next:

I am sitting here counting my blessings, so I am filled with joy. I have told you pieces of this story. However, God led me to write to you now before I forgot some things. . . .

I came home from the hospital on Friday, and somehow made it through Friday night. By Saturday night, things became very dark. About midnight, I sent my husband upstairs to the guest room because he could just not give me any comfort though he tried, and I wanted him to get some rest. . . .

I read my Bible, and God told me this was all for me. I finally received Jesus Christ and the Holy Spirit. God told me it had to happen this way. He told me I was His now, and that it was finished.

I began weeping with tears of great joy, and pure gratitude for every single agonizing moment since 12/05/2008 that it had taken to get me there, to get to God after all these years of searching. He has such perfect timing. . . . Those are the darkest and the most beautiful moments of my life. I had to be broken open to receive His Holy Spirit.

I raced up the stairs to my husband and woke him and he held me while I told Him what God had done.

I cannot believe what joy and contentment I feel now. It is so beautiful. I am His, and you helped to save me. I am His, and that is all I ever have to be.

Debbie later told me that she was one of those people who sat in the church pews for years believing she was a Christian, but she never really understood what she was hearing. She had never before made the decision to come to Jesus by faith and so had not experienced the joy of salvation.

Not everyone's story of faith is as dramatic as my friend Debbie's. However, I encourage you to take some time to consider your faith today. Christianity is more than a religion or something you do on Sunday. It's a life-changing relationship with Jesus. Don't settle for something less. Spend some time praying that the Lord would overwhelm you with joy that springs from your salvation.

Day 5: Devotional

We Need More Than a Spiritual Experience

However, do not rejoice that the spirits submit to you, but
rejoice that your names are written in heaven.

—Luke 10:20, niv

My friend Debbie came to our Bible study looking for some sort of spiritual experience. That's what our world often tells us is the key to finding joy and contentment, isn't it? Feeling anxious? Try meditation. Experiencing hardship? Try prayer. Feeling disconnected and melancholy? Try connecting with the divine.

However, these spiritual exercises are empty without the most important consideration: *Who is the object of your spiritual experience?* Who is it that you are praying to? Meditating on? Connecting with? The Hearer of our prayers is the substance of our hope. Any spiritual experience devoid of Jesus is an empty pursuit. We need something more than a spiritual experience. We need salvation.

Have you ever been rescued from a terrible fate and found yourself in a moment that could have changed everything? I have. Last fall I was driving on the highway when suddenly I lost control of my car. Something came apart in my front wheel, detaching it from the axle.

On my right loomed an eighteen-wheeler; on my left, the guardrail. Thankfully, the car veered left, careening into the guardrail at somewhere around seventy miles an hour. My car proceeded to spin 360 degrees with such force that the water bottle in my console spun through the air and was completely stripped of its plastic label. I came to a stop in the middle of the fast lane, bracing for the impact of another car.

It never came.

As I sat stunned in the front seat, I tried to move my car forward. I had no idea that both my front wheels were detached and pointed in opposite directions. Slowly, I opened the crushed driver's side door and squeezed out of the car.

A lady who stopped to help looked at me and said, "I saw the whole thing happen, and I didn't think anyone was getting out of that car." Tears of gratitude welled up, and I replied, "I thought the exact same thing." In the midst of an accident that takes only seconds, it's amazing how many thoughts you can think. My main thought was *This is it. I am going to die.*

When we know we've been rescued, we look at everything in a different light, don't we? I came home and hugged my husband and children a little tighter, ate my dinner with a deeper enjoyment, and experienced an overwhelming sense of gratitude. My thankfulness overflowed into joy, even in the most mundane of tasks.

This week we've spent our time studying both the author and some of the recipients of the letter to the Philippians. They each shared a common sense of deliverance. Paul was rescued from a life of persecuting the church. He moved swiftly from persecuting others to preaching the gospel to being persecuted himself.

While shackled in chains, he rejoiced. What could have brought such joy to his heart while enduring terrible pain and unjust circumstances? Paul understood that his spiritual rescue could never be taken from him. When everything else was dark, his salvation brought him joy.

The book of Philippians calls us to a life of joy. Here in Acts we see the source of all joy: our salvation. When the jailer came to belief, Luke recorded, "He was filled with joy because he had come to believe in God" (Acts 16:34, NIV).

Many people in our day are searching for joy through material possessions, fame, success, family, work, rest, spiritual experiences, or a variety of other earthly circumstances. In salvation, God gives us a joy that rests on something eternal, something stronger and more secure than anything on earth. Our joy rests in Jesus: His perfect life, His sacrificial death, His miraculous resurrection.

Once we believe in Jesus, we become children of God. We're rescued from our old way of life and brought into a new spiritual family. Even though we've made mistakes and even though we continue to struggle with sin, if we are in Christ, nothing can separate us from God's love. And if we are loved by an eternal God, we have an eternal source of joy available to us.

In Luke's gospel, we see Jesus emphasizing this truth. The disciples returned to Jesus rejoicing that God was working in and through them as they ministered to others. However, even when they were filled with enthusiasm, Jesus pointed them to a different source for joy: "Do not rejoice that the spirits submit to you, but rejoice that your names are written in heaven" (Luke 10:20, NIV).

Jesus faithfully reminded His followers that the basis of their joy was not their ministry success but the fact that God had rescued and redeemed them. Salvation is the greatest gift we can ever receive. Our rescue is the source of abundant joy.

You may be wondering, *What exactly have I been rescued from?* That's a really important question.

Since God is a good and just judge, every single misdeed that occurs must be punished. (A judge who didn't prosecute criminals would be neither good nor just.) The problem for each of us is that we've all done wrong things. We've all sinned and fallen short of God's standard. We deserve punishment. The bad news of our situation is very bad.

That's exactly what makes the good news so very good. Paul explained our miraculous rescue in his letter to the Romans:

> For while we were still weak, at the right time Christ died for the ungodly. For one will scarcely die for a righteous person—though perhaps for a good person one would dare even to die—but God shows his love for us in that while we were still sinners, Christ died for us. Since, therefore, we have now been justified by his blood, much more shall we be saved by him from the wrath of God. For if while we were enemies we were reconciled to God by the death of his Son, much more, now that we are reconciled, shall we be saved by his life. (5:6–10)

We've been rescued from the punishment we rightly earned. Whatever you think might be too big or too bad, Jesus paid the price. If you put your faith in Jesus, nothing you've done can keep you from His love. We're adopted into the family of God (Galatians 4:5). He calls us His children. He promises a home in heaven and eternal life.

Jesus knew the payment required to have our names written in the book of life. The cost of salvation was a debt you or I could never pay. We couldn't rescue ourselves. Only Jesus could. He willingly went to the cross on our behalf. When we forget that we've been rescued—when we forget the cross—we lose our joy.

As historic British minister Matthew Mead aptly stated,

> A name in heaven is only the portion of a few, and a special privilege and cause of rejoicing indeed. We are his adopted children. What greater ground of joy imaginable is there than this? With God as our portion, all he is and all he has is our inheritance. We have title to all our Father's riches and honours. God is our Father forever. How we should rejoice in this! To be a son or daughter of God, our everlasting Father, is the highest title in the world.[1]

I hope you'll pause now to consider what God has done to bring you to faith. Take time to rejoice in your rescue. If you've never believed in Christ, do not delay in giving your heart to God—nothing else will satisfy the longing in your soul. Talk to a trusted, believing friend or pray this simple prayer: "Lord, I want to know You. Open my eyes to the truth of the gospel, and give me salvation in Jesus. Rescue me and fill me with the joy of Your salvation. Amen."

A Shared Joy

Joy in True Fellowship

Philippians 1:1–11

Christ, who said to the disciples "Ye have not chosen me, but I have chosen you," can truly say to every group of Christian friends "You have not chosen one another but I have chosen you for one another." The Friendship is not a reward for our discrimination and good taste in finding one another out. It is the instrument by which God reveals to each the beauties of all the others.

—C. S. Lewis

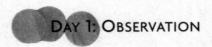

DAY 1: OBSERVATION

What Does the Text Say?

December is my favorite month of the year to open my mailbox. I go expectantly, hoping for more than the usual junk mail and bills. Each day cards arrive from friends and family all over the world. With excitement I open the letters, giving thanks for each person.

It's a delight to have friends, isn't it? Sometimes I haven't seen certain faces for years, but it's always a joy to reconnect, even if it's just through a picture on a Christmas card.

This week we'll be looking at Philippians 1:1–11, specifically considering the fellowship that bound Paul in such a loving way with those at the church in Philippi. But for right now, I want you to take out your Bible (or you can look in the back of this study if you don't have your Bible with you) and open it to the book of Philippians.

Imagine the mail carrier just dropped this letter on your doorstep. Sit down with a cup of hot coffee or tea (my favorite) and read the entire book. It won't take long. Just read it once through and take in Paul's words with the expectancy of getting a long-awaited letter in the mail.

As you read Philippians, does any particular verse encourage you or stand out to you? Write down that verse and note why it spoke to you today.

Now take a few minutes to reread **Philippians 1:1–11.**

> ¹Paul and Timothy, servants of Christ Jesus,
>
> To all the saints in Christ Jesus who are at Philippi, with the overseers and deacons:
>
> ²Grace to you and peace from God our Father and the Lord Jesus Christ.

³I thank my God in all my remembrance of you, ⁴always in every prayer of mine for you all making my prayer with joy, ⁵because of your partnership in the gospel from the first day until now. ⁶And I am sure of this, that he who began a good work in you will bring it to completion at the day of Jesus Christ. ⁷It is right for me to feel this way about you all, because I hold you in my heart, for you are all partakers with me of grace, both in my imprisonment and in the defense and confirmation of the gospel. ⁸For God is my witness, how I yearn for you all with the affection of Christ Jesus. ⁹And it is my prayer that your love may abound more and more, with knowledge and all discernment, ¹⁰so that you may approve what is excellent, and so be pure and blameless for the day of Christ, ¹¹filled with the fruit of righteousness that comes through Jesus Christ, to the glory and praise of God.

1. While the letter is formally attributed to Paul and Timothy, it is understood by New Testament scholars that Paul wrote the letter and that Timothy was with him as he wrote. What title did Paul give himself and Timothy?

2. How did Paul address the Philippians? What did he call them?

3. What words of blessing did he use to greet them (verse 2)?

4. How did Paul remember the Philippians (verse 3)?

5. What attitude did Paul have as he prayed? What explanation did he give for this?

6. Regarding the Philippians, what was Paul confident of? What was the basis for his confidence?

7. What do we learn in this passage about Paul's personal circumstances?

8. What did Paul pray for in verse 9?

9. Why did he pray this? List four reasons (verses 10–11).

It's clear from the beginning of his letter that Paul wrote to the Philippians with deep affection. He was thankful for them. He prayed for them. He yearned for them. And so he wrote to them.

This letter has traveled across generations and landed at your doorstep. It's been preserved, translated, and delivered to you. And Paul's words are full of meaning for you today. The Bible's relevance through all generations testifies to its true authorship: God. Somehow the Lord has put this letter in your hands today. What a gift to receive a letter from God.

I hope and pray the Lord will bring you each day to the book of Philippians with the same sort of excitement that propels me to my mailbox in December. Close your time today asking God to fill you with wonder and expectation as you read His Word in this study. These are not just Paul's words to the Philippians; these are God's words to you.

DAY 2: INTERPRETATION

What Does the Text Mean?

Today we'll dig a little deeper into this first section of Philippians. Yesterday we observed the passage; now we'll begin the work of interpreting it. Take time to read carefully, thoughtfully, expectantly. Don't rush. Enjoy this time—just as your body needs exercise, your soul needs God's Word. Whatever is clamoring for your time and energy will still be there after you read.

All relationships take time, including our relationship with God. The twenty to thirty minutes you spend now will fill your heart and mind with truth that will sustain and encourage you. As the British preacher John Blanchard wrote,

> How often do we face problems, temptation and pressure? *Every day!*
> Then how often do we need instruction, guidance and greater encourage-
> ment? *Every day!* To catch all these felt needs up into an even greater issue,
> how often do we need to see God's face, hear his voice, feel his touch,
> know his power? The answer to all these questions is the same: *every day!*[1]

We need time with Jesus every day. Begin today with prayer, asking God to give you understanding and insight.

Turn to pages 36–37 and read **Philippians 1:1–11.**

1. Why do you think Paul described himself as a servant in verse 1? Why not as an apostle, leader, or founder of the church in Philippi?

2. Read the verses below and answer the questions that follow.

But Aaron and his sons made offerings on the altar of burnt offering and on the altar of incense for all the work of the Most Holy Place, and to make atonement for Israel, according to all that Moses the servant of God had commanded. (1 Chronicles 6:49)

After these things Joshua the son of Nun, the servant of the LORD, died, being 110 years old. (Joshua 24:29)

To the choirmaster. Of David, the servant of the LORD. (Psalm 36, title)

And Mary said, "Behold, I am the servant of the Lord; let it be to me according to your word." And the angel departed from her. (Luke 1:38)

a. What word is used to describe these believers similarly to how Paul described himself?

b. What key difference do you notice?

3. What did Paul mean by the terms *overseers* and *deacons*? (See 1 Timothy 3 for an explanation of these roles.) What does this greeting tell you about the size of the church in Philippi?

4. The biblical word *grace* is often defined as "unmerited favor" or "demerited favor." (Not only do we fail to earn God's favor, but we actually deserve God's punishment.) Describe how grace comes to us from God through Christ.

5. *Peace* can mean either "freedom from disturbance; quiet and tranquility" or "freedom from or the cessation of war or violence."[2] What does peace look like for us as Christians? How does God give us peace in Christ?

6. Why do you think Paul's memories of the Philippians brought him joy? Think back to Acts 16. During his time in Philippi, he was beaten and put in jail. While all his circumstances were not joyful, what gave him joy?

7. Overall, how would you describe Paul's feelings toward the Philippians? What words or phrases help you come to that conclusion?

8. Paul took joy in their fellowship because of their partnership in the gospel. What's the difference between friendship and partnership in the gospel? Are they mutually exclusive? Explain your answer.

9. Why was Paul confident that God, who began a good work in them, would bring it to completion?

10. Often how we pray for someone speaks to our greatest hope for that person. What was Paul hoping for as he prayed for the Philippians?

11. Ultimately, why did Paul want them to be pure and blameless, filled with the fruit of righteousness?

12. How does an increase in our knowledge of God lead to greater discernment, purity, and righteousness?

In his introduction, Paul identified himself as a *servant* of Christ Jesus and he wrote to the *saints* in Christ Jesus. His word choice here is significant on both counts. All throughout the Old Testament, the leaders of the Israelites were given the distinction of being called *servants of God*.

When Paul introduced himself, he made one slight change. Did you notice it?

Paul didn't call himself a servant of God or a servant of the Lord. He said he was a servant of Christ Jesus. This word choice has an important implication: *he equated Jesus with God.*

While this might be old news to you and me, it's significant from a historical perspective that Paul believed Jesus and God are the same. The understanding that Jesus is God isn't a legend that developed hundreds of years after His death, when people had forgotten the real person. Those who followed Him and knew Him personally believed Jesus was both fully God and fully man.

It's also encouraging to note that Paul addressed the Philippians as *saints*. In fact, this is the term he regularly used in his letters when referring to fellow believers.

Once we're part of the family of God, we're considered saints, not sinners. (Paul never wrote to the "sinners in Rome" or anywhere else for that matter.)

Being a saint doesn't mean we're perfect. It's who we become when we believe. Our identity doesn't mean we are free from our fight against sin. We'll make mistakes all our lives. However, there's a big difference between being a saint who struggles with sin and being a sinner who's trying to be a saint.

Be encouraged today: you're a beloved saint of God! You may not feel like one, but your identity is unchanging, rooted in God's disposition toward you. By faith in Jesus, we're adopted by God and we're part of His family.

Spend some time in prayer, asking God to renew and refresh your heart with this good news. It's easy to become discouraged by mistakes and failures. Certainly we should rightly mourn and confess our sin. But we also need to rejoice in our new identity. Go to the Lord now, freely, expectantly, boldly, and full of hope. He sees you as His child, and you can bring all your hopes, fears, and failures to Him.

DAY 3: INTERPRETATION

What Does the Text Mean?

Friendship is important. Whether we have many friends or keep a few close ones, we need one another for support, encouragement, challenge, and perspective. Friendships influence the choices we make and how we experience joys and sorrows. It's vital that our connections be based on something more significant than just a desire for friendship. As C. S. Lewis explained,

> The very condition of having Friends is that we should want something else besides Friends. Where the truthful answer to the question *Do you see the same truth?* would be "I see nothing and I don't care about the truth; I only want a Friend," no Friendship can arise—though Affection of course may. There would be nothing for the Friendship to be *about;* and Friendship must be about something, even if it were only an enthusiasm for dominoes or white mice. Those who have nothing can share nothing; those who are going nowhere can have no fellow-travellers.[3]

Paul's friendship with the Philippians was rooted in their shared identity and mission. This relationship brought him great joy and thanksgiving. To help us gain a better understanding of biblical friendship, we'll spend our time today looking up other verses that teach about friendship. These passages help identify healthy patterns in friendships and how we can find true partners in the gospel.

1. Read the following verses and underline the benefit of friendships mentioned in each passage.

   a. Ecclesiastes 4:9–12

   [9]Two are better than one, because they have a good reward for their toil. [10]For if they fall, one will lift up his fellow. But woe to him who is alone when he falls and has not another to lift him up! [11]Again, if two lie together, they keep warm, but how can one keep warm alone? [12]And though a man might prevail against one who is alone, two will withstand him—a threefold cord is not quickly broken.

   b. Proverbs 27:6

   Faithful are the wounds of a friend;
      profuse are the kisses of an enemy.

c. Proverbs 27:9

Oil and perfume make the heart glad,
    and the sweetness of a friend comes from his earnest counsel.

d. Proverbs 27:17

Iron sharpens iron,
    and one man sharpens another.

How would you summarize the benefits of friendship as revealed in these verses?

2. The Bible also gives us warnings about friendships. Read the following verses and note what they advise about forming friendships.

a. Proverbs 12:26

One who is righteous is a guide to his neighbor,
    but the way of the wicked leads them astray.

b. Proverbs 22:24–25

Make no friendship with a man given to anger,
    nor go with a wrathful man,
lest you learn his ways
    and entangle yourself in a snare.

c. Proverbs 19:4

Wealth brings many new friends,
    but a poor man is deserted by his friend.

d. Proverbs 19:6

Many seek the favor of a generous man,
    and everyone is a friend to a man who gives gifts.

According to these verses, what concerns should we keep in mind regarding friendship?

3. What friendships in your own life have helped you to know Jesus more? When has a friendship had a negative impact on your faith?

4. What sort of influence does your friendship have on others? What do you observe in Paul's friendship with the Philippians that encourages you in your friendship with others? What can you glean from his example?

Since my teen years, the Lord has blessed me with friends who love Jesus. In high school, my friend Holley and I planned ministry events and Bible studies together. In college, my roommate Beth and I led a small group in our dorm. Since then, I've led neighborhood Bible studies, planned ministry events, and taught Sunday school alongside a variety of women. In fact, this study is in your hands today because of a friendship!

Each of these experiences taught me an important lesson. Friendship blossoms in the soil where we plant ourselves and spend our time. If we spend our days at work, we'll make friendships there. If we stay at home raising children, we'll develop friendships with other moms with similarly aged children. If we love a sports team, we'll make friends who share the same passion.

We build relationship around shared pursuits. If you want to build deeper Christian friendships (and I hope you do), I encourage you to get involved in your church. Serving as a Bible study leader, in the nursery, on the hospitality team, or on the budget committee is a great way to build relationships. Find what you love to do, and do it with others. And most important, by gathering together every Sunday to give praise to God and hear the Word preached, we enter into the deepest kind of fellowship with those sitting around us.

Of course, it's important to develop relationships outside the church. Jesus did that as well—He dined with tax collectors and sinners. However, He spent the majority of His time with the disciples. He traveled with them, ministered with them, and prayed with them. It's vital that we're rooted deeply with those who share our passion for the gospel, partnering with them to serve Jesus.

One of the most important reasons we need Christian friends is because of the advice and wisdom they share. So many voices are speaking to us—the television, the internet, entertainment and celebrity culture, and books and magazines. Like a map that's turned upside down, many of these point us in precisely the wrong direction to find contentment and joy. They tell us that if we were thinner or more successful or had just the right hair product, then all would be well. We need friendships that are centered on God's Word to speak above the cultural clamor.

Proverbs 27:9 speaks of the sweetness that comes from the wise counsel of a friend. These friends love us enough to tell us the truth, even when doing so might be uncomfortable for them and for us. But I've found this to be true in life: it's the friends willing to call me out on my sin and say hard things whom I trust the most. They're the ones I return to time and again for advice and wisdom—precisely because they recognize I'm a work in progress. Thankfully, they're willing to help guide me when I need it most.

Close your time in prayer today, asking the Lord to allow you to be a friend who gives earnest and good counsel and to give you friends who do the same.

Day 4: Application

How Does the Text Transform Me?

I met my friend Angela over fifteen years ago. Originally, another friend referred her to me as a wonderful babysitter. Over the years our friendship grew, even though we were in completely different seasons of life. She was single and enrolled in seminary, while I was married and mothering young children. Our lives didn't naturally intersect, but we both shared a passion for Bible study and teaching.

Throughout the years, we worked on a variety of ministry endeavors together. At one point, we spent hours developing a study on the Ten Commandments, which we then taught at our church. Serving together bonded our hearts. As we wrote and worked, we also shared life and laughter. We prayed for each other. We chatted about all of life, not just ministry. I listened to her as she worked through singleness and seminary, and she listened to me as I struggled with discipline and diapers.

Our lives became entwined not because of seasons or circumstances but because of shared partnership in the gospel. Our unity in Christ has allowed us to remain good friends even as our circumstances have changed. Currently, she spends her days mothering her three small boys, while I spend my days writing and working.

Can I tell you what a joy her friendship is to me? Our connection is deeper and richer because it's rooted in something more than us. When I think of a true partner in the gospel, I think of Angela. I hold her as a sister in my heart, always wanting the best for her. I pray for her—that her love for God will abound more and more in love and depth of insight.

As we dig into the opening verses of Philippians again, listen for Paul's deep love and affection for his readers. It's a beautiful picture of what we as Christians can be to one another. Begin your time in prayer, asking God to give you wisdom and insight as you read and seek to apply this passage to your own life.

Turn to pages 36–37 and read **Philippians 1:1–11**.

1. Paul introduced himself as a servant of Christ Jesus. He called the Philippian believers "saints in Christ Jesus." He defined himself and

others by their relationship with Christ. Nothing else was more important. Think through all that this world defines people by: job title, income
level, family pedigree, children, spouse, appearance, education level, and a
myriad of other factors. Often we begin to measure our worth and find
our significance in these areas instead of in the simple fact that we are
each a child of God and loved by Him.

a. Where are you tempted to find your significance outside of Jesus?
   What makes you feel important and worthy of love?

b. Some of us, at times, fail to believe we are significant or important at
   all. Perhaps we feel that we are less important than everyone around
   us. How does Paul's description of himself as a servant and of his
   recipients as saints give you hope? What personal encouragement do
   you find in the words of Jesus in Matthew 23:11: "The greatest among
   you shall be your servant"?

2. As noted earlier, *grace* can be defined as "unmerited favor," while *peace*
   is defined as "freedom from disturbance; quiet and tranquility." God's
   unmerited favor toward us yields peace in our hearts. What do you feel
   anxious about today? In what ways is your heart not at peace?

3. Read **Philippians 4:6–7.**

⁶Do not be anxious about anything, but in everything by prayer and supplication with thanksgiving let your requests be made known to God. ⁷And the peace of God, which surpasses all understanding, will guard your hearts and your minds in Christ Jesus.

a. What did Paul encourage the Philippians to do when they felt anxious?

b. Describe a time when prayer led you to feel at peace.

4. Do you feel at peace with God today? Do you believe His grace is upon you? Why or why not?

Knowing we've received God's grace allows us to experience a different sort of peace. Coming to faith doesn't mean we experience freedom from trials and hardships. In fact, sometimes our faith puts us in harm's way.

Paul wrote this letter from jail. He knew what it was to suffer as a Christian. However, he experienced peace in the midst of earthly suffering because of the heavenly assurance that grace supplies. Whatever may happen in this world, our destiny and identity are secure. We face momentary trials, but an eternity of joy in Christ's presence awaits. One day He will wipe away your tears—there will be no more death, no more pain, no more suffering.

Today you may have concerns that make you anxious. You likely face circumstances you can't control. You struggle under the weight of everything you have to do. I feel these pressures as well. Yet we can face today with peace and joy because something better is coming. When all around us seems bleak, we can look ahead to the promise of what will be. We're on the journey now, but He's bringing us home. One day all will be made right.

Thankfully, He gives us fellow travelers on our journey. Just as Paul was heartened by the Philippians, we can find encouragement from one another as we walk with God.

5. Think back over your life. Which individuals do you remember with thanksgiving? Why?

6. Paul took joy in the Philippians because of their partnership in the gospel. When have you experienced this type of fellowship with others as you have served together? How has that led to joy in your friendships?

7. Paul declared with assurance, "He who began a good work in you will bring it to completion" (1:6). How does this promise encourage you today?

8. My own prayers tend to be focused on the circumstances of life. (*Please help Ann to get well. Please help Sarah's house to sell.* And so on.) These are good things to pray for, and we are invited to bring any and all requests to God. However, Paul prayed for things broader than immediate circumstances. How does his prayer for the Philippians encourage you to pray differently?

9. Paul longed for his readers to grow in knowledge and depth of insight. If someone asked you, "How do I grow in knowledge and discernment?" what would you tell that person? What has most deepened your own understanding of God?

10. What would it look like for your love for others and for God to abound more and more?

11. As you consider the words of this passage, what particular application resonates in your heart and mind today? What specifically do you need to believe or do in light of Philippians 1:1–11?

One thing that strikes me about Paul's affection for the Philippians is that it naturally overflowed in prayers for them. He prayed frequently, confidently, and lovingly. His assurance of God's work within them didn't diminish his prayers for them; rather, it caused him to pray with all the more confidence.

One of the most loving ways we can care for others is to pray for them. Just this week a friend emailed me to ask for prayer. She feared she was miscarrying. (She'd already lost three babies to miscarriage, so she was painfully aware of the signs.) She lives far away, so I couldn't be there with her. However, through prayer I could join with her and share in the privilege of calling out to God on her behalf.

Later that afternoon I received a follow-up email from her—the ultrasound revealed a healthy baby with a strong heartbeat! Just as I had shared in her concern, now I could share in her joy. I rejoiced with her in God's kindness and turned my prayers to thanksgiving on her behalf.

Prayer unites us with others. It allows us to share both joys and sorrows. I encourage you to sit for a few minutes and ask the Lord to bring to mind someone who needs prayer today. As you pray, remember that person with thanksgiving. And if you can, tell your friend you prayed for her. Hopefully it will encourage her and spur her on in her own prayer life.

We never know what the Lord might be accomplishing with our prayers.

DAY 5: DEVOTIONAL

The Beauty of True Fellowship

Oil and perfume make the heart glad,
and the sweetness of a friend comes from his earnest counsel.

—PROVERBS 27:9

These words from the fictional Anne Shirley in *Anne of Green Gables* capture our deep desire for friendship:

"Marilla, . . . do you think that I shall ever have a bosom friend in Avonlea?"

"A—a what kind of friend?"

"A bosom friend—an intimate friend, you know—a really kindred spirit to whom I can confide my inmost soul. I've dreamed of meeting her all my life. I never really supposed I would, but so many of my loveliest dreams have come true all at once that perhaps this one will, too. Do you think it's possible?"[4]

As Anne expressed, it's a sweet gift to have people in our lives who love us and whom we love. From the very beginning, God created each of us with a need for companionship. Even surrounded by the perfection of Eden, it wasn't good for Adam to be alone. To fulfill Adam's need for a suitable companion and to make all things very good, God created Eve. However, since sin entered the picture, all our relationships have suffered.

To fulfill our need for fellowship, we often unite around shared passions or activities. Some find unity in sports teams, fraternities, sororities, or college alumni associations. Others find friendship in professional organizations, work colleagues, service clubs, or neighborhood associations. Each of us longs to fulfill our good desire for companionship.

In his letter to the Philippians, Paul highlighted the unity that leads to the greatest of joys. While many types of relationships may give us friendship, he spoke of a depth of affection and unity that supersedes other types of companionship. Paul delighted in the satisfaction that comes from true fellowship. This joy flows from three truths: a shared identity in Christ, a partnership in the gospel, and a unified hope for the future.

Paul's fellowship with the Philippians began with a shared identity. Paul referred to himself as a servant of Christ and addressed the Philippians as "saints in Christ." Their unity was not formed from an earthly association but a heavenly one. Consider this motley crew: Paul, Timothy, Lydia, the jailer, and the slave woman from Philippi. Whatever their differences—gender, profession, social standing, race, or religious upbringing—they were linked together in Jesus. Their primary identity was in the saving mercies of Christ. The root of their fellowship determined the quality and sweetness of the fruit.

Second, Paul's affection for the Philippians flowed out of a shared calling to partner in the gospel. While each person may have labored in a different way, they all labored for a common purpose. They partnered together for God's kingdom and His glory.

Our desire for fellowship will most often find satisfaction in shared ministry with others. As we partner in the gospel, a deep and abiding affection grows. If you feel lonely or devoid of companionship, let me encourage you to consider volunteering in your local church or another organization in which you can work alongside those who share your joy in demonstrating the love of Christ.

Our friendships in the church will most likely still suffer from selfishness and sin. Christians aren't perfect. Our friends may disappoint us. However, the church is our best hope for finding the type of partnership Paul found with the Philippians. Don't settle for less. Our work together in the gospel leads to deep affection and shared joy.

Lastly, Paul's joy was rooted and grounded in prayer. Paul focused his hopes for the Philippians on something more than earthly circumstances. He faithfully prayed for them, that their love for God would abound more and more in depth of insight. He hoped that the fruit of this love would be discernment, purity, and righteousness, all to the glory of God. He wanted *more* for them and knew that fullness in life comes through Christ alone.

Our faithfulness to pray for our friends is often directly correlated to our affection for them. Prayer warms the heart and grows our love for others. Consider your friendships right now. Who needs your faithful prayers today? Join Paul in praying these words:

> And it is my prayer that your love may abound more and more, with
> knowledge and all discernment, so that you may approve what is
> excellent, and so be pure and blameless for the day of Christ, filled with
> the fruit of righteousness that comes through Jesus Christ, to the glory
> and praise of God. (Philippians 1:9–11)

In Christ we have union, partnership in purpose, and prayer that links us through time and eternity as the people of God. Our relationship with Christ overflows into our fellowship with others. In a world where we can have hundreds of casual Facebook friends, what a gift to experience shared partnership that brings true joy.

Unshakeable

Joy in Christ's Lordship

Philippians 1:12–30

The doctrine of providence teaches Christians that they are never in the grip of blind forces (fortune, chance, luck, fate); all that happens to them is divinely planned, and each event comes as a new summons to trust, obey, and rejoice, knowing that all is for one's spiritual and eternal good.

—J. I. Packer

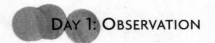

Day 1: Observation

What Does the Text Say?

Many of us equate the experience of joy and peace with a problem-free existence. If we could rid our lives of all inconveniences, hardships, and trials, then we'd find the elusive contentment we're searching for in life.

However, every life is touched by suffering. None of us are free from hardships. I'm sure, as you read these words, something weighs heavy on your heart. Perhaps a job situation is frustrating. Or a family member is sick. Perhaps a child is dealing with a problem that doesn't have any easy solutions. Or a move has left you lonely and hurting. Perhaps a relationship is broken. Maybe multiple things are happening all at once, and you wonder, *How can I bear all this? It's just too much.*

While these struggles may be surprising to us, they're no surprise to Jesus. He knew this world would be full of trials. And while He never promised us a pain-free existence, He did promise peace in the midst of our difficulties. He explained, "I have said these things to you, that in me you may have peace. In the world you will have tribulation. But take heart; I have overcome the world" (John 16:33).

This week we're going to explore a surprising place where Paul found joy—in his sufferings. It wasn't the trials that made Paul rejoice but the knowledge that God was in control of every circumstance he endured. He recognized that our God is Lord of all and that, whatever happens, He reigns over all things well, even the painful trials.

I'll admit, this isn't an easy chapter to write. It's an even more difficult truth to live. I'm writing these words while wearing a cast on my broken ankle, enduring an unexplainable itchy rash all over my face, and dealing with a child who has lice. It's not what I'd choose for myself today.

That's why it's good news that God is in control and we aren't. Sometimes hard things are good for us in ways we can't understand. We have limited vision, but God exists outside of time and space. He's weaving together a beautiful tapestry, even though in our eyes it sometimes seems like a jumbled mess.

What seems unclear today will one day come into focus. Then we'll understand and rejoice in all He has done. Believing this truth and learning to hope in God's good plan, even when we can't see its goodness, opens our hearts to rejoice in God when we're going through life's greatest difficulties. We become women who are "sorrowful, yet always rejoicing" (2 Corinthians 6:10).

Today, we'll finish Philippians chapter 1. To begin, we'll consider some background information. After Paul's second missionary journey in Acts 16, which we studied in week 1, he went on a third journey, taking the time to visit the Philippians once again (Acts 20:6).

When Paul returned to Jerusalem, his faithful preaching of the gospel angered the Jewish leaders. He was arrested and sent to Felix, the governor (Acts 23), who kept him imprisoned for almost two years. The Jewish leaders continued to seek his death, so eventually Paul, a Roman citizen, appealed to Caesar. This began his long journey to Rome.

At each step along the way, Paul had opportunities to share the gospel with his captors: Governor Felix, King Agrippa, the native people of Malta (due to a shipwreck on the journey), and the Jewish leaders in Rome. He spent two years in Rome under house arrest and was allowed to preach to and teach all who came to him during his time there (Acts 28:16, 30–31). It is believed this letter to the Philippians was written during Paul's house arrest in Rome, sometime around AD 62.

Keeping in mind that backstory, read **Philippians 1:12–30.**

> [12]I want you to know, brothers, that what has happened to me has really served to advance the gospel, [13]so that it has become known throughout the whole imperial guard and to all the rest that my imprisonment is for Christ. [14]And most of the brothers, having become confident in the Lord by my imprisonment, are much more bold to speak the word without fear.
>
> [15]Some indeed preach Christ from envy and rivalry, but others from good will. [16]The latter do it out of love, knowing that I am put here for the defense of the gospel. [17]The former proclaim Christ out of selfish ambition, not sincerely but thinking to afflict me in my imprisonment.

[18]What then? Only that in every way, whether in pretense or in truth, Christ is proclaimed, and in that I rejoice.

Yes, and I will rejoice, [19]for I know that through your prayers and the help of the Spirit of Jesus Christ this will turn out for my deliverance, [20]as it is my eager expectation and hope that I will not be at all ashamed, but that with full courage now as always Christ will be honored in my body, whether by life or by death. [21]For to me to live is Christ, and to die is gain. [22]If I am to live in the flesh, that means fruitful labor for me. Yet which I shall choose I cannot tell. [23]I am hard pressed between the two. My desire is to depart and be with Christ, for that is far better. [24]But to remain in the flesh is more necessary on your account. [25]Convinced of this, I know that I will remain and continue with you all, for your progress and joy in the faith, [26]so that in me you may have ample cause to glory in Christ Jesus, because of my coming to you again.

[27]Only let your manner of life be worthy of the gospel of Christ, so that whether I come and see you or am absent, I may hear of you that you are standing firm in one spirit, with one mind striving side by side for the faith of the gospel, [28]and not frightened in anything by your opponents. This is a clear sign to them of their destruction, but of your salvation, and that from God. [29]For it has been granted to you that for the sake of Christ you should not only believe in him but also suffer for his sake, [30]engaged in the same conflict that you saw I had and now hear that I still have.

1. According to the summary provided before the passage, what were some of the difficult circumstances that happened to Paul? What three effects did they yield (verses 12–14)?

2. What two reasons are given for why some preached Christ? How did Paul respond to each?

3. What two reasons did Paul give for his rejoicing (verses 18–19)?

4. What did Paul eagerly expect and hope for (verse 20)?

5. What two options did he set forth for his deliverance?

6. What benefits did Paul anticipate would come from his continuing to live? If he were to die?

7. What was his hope for the Philippians (verses 25–26)?

8. How did he exhort them to conduct themselves (verse 27)?

9. If they walked in a manner worthy of the gospel, what three effects would result?

10. What two things had been granted to the Philippians for the sake of
    Christ?

In this passage we see Paul rejoicing despite multiple personal hardships. He
was imprisoned, ministry rivals were preaching with wrong motives, and he was
aware that he may be put to death for his faith.

In the midst of these struggles, Paul took comfort in God's plan. He understood his imprisonment had a larger purpose. While some preached from envy and
rivalry, hoping to afflict Paul in his imprisonment, he rejoiced because Christ was
being proclaimed. When facing the reality he might die for his faith, Paul was confident that whatever happened would be for his gain and God's glory.

Paul's life is a beautiful testimony to what happens when we trust God is faithfully reigning over all things. Many people speak of this concept as Christ's
lordship—that God is at work in every detail, in every circumstance. Not a single
molecule exists outside His domain. Not a hair could fall from Paul's head without
God's knowledge. Paul's understanding of Christ's lordship allowed him to patiently endure hardship.

Today, I expect you are facing hardship and trials of some sort. Whatever you
are experiencing, I encourage you to pray. We can ask God to remove the trial. He
is able to work in ways we can't even imagine.

However, sometimes it is for our good that the trial remains. As Puritan
preacher Thomas Watson wrote, "If the thing we desire be good for us, we shall
have it; if it be not good, then the not having is good for us."[1]

Pause now and ask for a heart that trusts God's plan. Ask that whatever happens you might live worthy of the gospel of Christ, that your life might shine the
hope of the gospel in a worn and weary world.

Take courage; this is our God:

> Now to him who is able to do far more abundantly than all that we ask
> or think, according to the power at work within us, to him be glory in
> the church and in Christ Jesus throughout all generations, forever and
> ever. Amen. (Ephesians 3:20–21)

Day 2: Interpretation

What Does the Text Mean?

In week 1, I shared about my friend Debbie's battle with cancer. She fought bravely for five years. Eventually, the cancer returned, and we knew that without a miracle, it would take her life.

Debbie's medical journey and her spiritual journey were intricately intertwined. We prayed together, wept together, laughed together, celebrated good news, and mourned difficult news. Through it all, her greatest hope was to tell others about the love of Christ.

The only regret I ever heard her express was that she hadn't developed a personal relationship with Jesus at an earlier age. At our last Bible study together, she said two things I've never forgotten. We were studying the story of Cornelius in Acts 10 and all God had done to bring him to faith. As we talked about the different ways the Lord had worked in our lives, Debbie said, "God used my cancer to bring me to faith." Without a hint of bitterness, full of joy, she continued, "And it's all been worth it. If it took cancer for me to know Jesus, then that is all that matters."

In her suffering, Debbie's faith shone. As her body failed, her countenance glowed with an indescribable beauty. Her deep trust in God's plan for her life reminds me of Paul's faith.

Today we'll read the same section again, considering what the text means. Read the passage carefully, giving yourself time to reflect on the words and the meaning behind Paul's words.

Turn to pages 59–60 and read **Philippians 1:12–30**.

1. Why do you think Paul wanted to tell the Philippians about the blessings that came from his imprisonment?

2. As a result of Paul's imprisonment, why would most of the brothers be bolder to speak about Christ without fear? Wouldn't you expect Paul's imprisonment to make them *more* fearful? See Acts 4:23–31.

3. Why would envy and rivalry propel people to preach Christ? What do you think they might have been hoping to gain?

4. How did their success in preaching Christ (even with incorrect motives) affect Paul?

5. Paul's outward circumstances were difficult. How would you describe his inward condition? What clues in the text support your conclusions?

6. What advantages did Paul cite for living? For dying?

7. What would it look like for the Philippians to experience "progress and joy in the faith"?

8. What would it look like to live worthy of the gospel of Christ? Read **Galatians 5:16–24** and on the following page list the contrasts between the life lived by the Spirit and the life lived by the flesh.

[16]But I say, walk by the Spirit, and you will not gratify the desires of the flesh. [17]For the desires of the flesh are against the Spirit, and the desires of the Spirit are against the flesh, for these are opposed to each other, to keep you from doing the things you want to do. [18]But if you are led by the Spirit, you are not under the law. [19]Now the works of the flesh are evident: sexual immorality, impurity, sensuality, [20]idolatry, sorcery, enmity, strife, jealousy, fits of anger, rivalries, dissensions, divisions, [21]envy, drunkenness, orgies, and things like these. I warn you, as I warned you before, that those who do such things will not inherit the kingdom of God. [22]But the fruit of the Spirit is love, joy, peace, patience, kindness, goodness, faithfulness, [23]gentleness, self-control; against such things there is no law. [24]And those who belong to Christ Jesus have crucified the flesh with its passions and desires.

Life by the Spirit   **Life by the Flesh**

9. How would living by the Spirit enhance their unity and dispel fear?

10. Why did Paul say it had been "granted" to the Philippians for them to suffer for the gospel as though it were a blessing? Is suffering for Christ a blessing? Explain your answer.

Do you find Paul's words surprising? He didn't fret over other people's wrong motives in ministry. He wasn't worried about his own safety. His vision was set on something greater. His spiritual eyes looked for the good that God was accomplishing through the trials he faced. Whatever happened, his ultimate goal was to honor Christ, whether in life or in death.

My friend Debbie lived in light of these truths until the day she died. Oh, how she wanted to be healed and tell her story of God's rescue. She wanted to see her children grow up and to be there for all the milestones—graduations, weddings, grandchildren. Yet God had other plans. Cancer robbed her body of its strength, but it didn't rob Debbie of life. Her flesh failed, but her soul is safe for eternity.

Months before her death, Debbie asked me to speak at her funeral. She wanted me to share the gospel with everyone who came. When the time came, through tears I recounted God's work in Debbie's life. I also shared a poem I wrote in Debbie's last days. It was both my prayer for Debbie and my way of trusting God's plan for her life.

A Song for Debbie

The clouds have come, the storm winds blow;
With sadness, I realize it's time for you to go.
Release, release, release, cries my soul—
Abandon these shadows and become whole.

Walk in newness, with all made right,
In safe pasture where there is no night.
Pain be gone and with it tears,
No more mourning, no more fears.

Jesus is there, waiting for you,
Drying your eyes, making all things new.

Yet, I must walk in these Shadow Lands,
Missing my friend, not always understanding His plans.
In this darkness am I, yet not alone,
Waiting for the day Christ calls me home.

For then together, we all will be
Laughing and rejoicing, able to see:
That all He has done has been done in love.
His plans make sense when seen from above.

Until that reunion day so sweet,
We must carry on, being His hands, His feet,
Going to the places you wanted to go,
Spreading His gospel, letting people know:

Death does not win, hope is real;
In the wounds of Christ, our God will heal.

So today I mourn, but mourn in hope,
Asking for faith to give my vision broader scope.
On this side of eternity, I miss you, my friend—
Sweet Debbie, may you rest in joy without end.

Whatever you face today, redemption will come. One day we will understand the abundant goodness of God's plan. This future hope gives us present joy.

Take your burdens, heartaches, and struggles to the Lord today. Pour out your heart to Him in prayer. Don't lean on your own understanding. Trust in Him. Choose to rejoice in what is good, even as you mourn what is hard.

Day 3: Interpretation

What Does the Text Mean?

In the passage we've been studying the past two days, Paul shared about his own suffering, and he encouraged the Philippians to walk in a manner worthy of the gospel in their trials. Today we'll look at some other passages in Scripture that deal with hardships so that we can gain greater insight into the role of suffering in our lives.

We face a variety of trials. It might be lack of sleep, health problems, financial problems, anxiety, relational discord, depression, or loneliness—each of us deals with hardship at some level. These verses give us a window into God's purposes and plans for suffering. He doesn't waste it.

1. As you read the following verses, underline what you learn about suffering. Then specifically think through the question that follows, writing your conclusions in the space provided.

   a. Romans 5:1–5

   [1]Therefore, since we have been justified by faith, we have peace with God through our Lord Jesus Christ. [2]Through him we have also obtained access by faith into this grace in which we stand, and we rejoice in hope of the glory of God. [3]Not only that, but we rejoice in our sufferings, knowing that suffering produces endurance, [4]and endurance produces character, and character produces hope, [5]and hope does not put us to shame, because God's love has been poured into our hearts through the Holy Spirit who has been given to us.

   b. 1 Peter 1:6–7

   [6]In this you rejoice, though now for a little while, if necessary, you have been grieved by various trials, [7]so that the tested genuineness of your faith—more precious than gold that perishes though it is tested by fire—may be found to result in praise and glory and honor at the revelation of Jesus Christ.

   c. 2 Corinthians 1:5–11

   [5]For as we share abundantly in Christ's sufferings, so through Christ we share abundantly in comfort too. [6]If we are afflicted, it is for your comfort and salvation; and if we are comforted, it is for your comfort,

which you experience when you patiently endure the same sufferings that we suffer. ⁷Our hope for you is unshaken, for we know that as you share in our sufferings, you will also share in our comfort.

⁸For we do not want you to be unaware, brothers, of the affliction we experienced in Asia. For we were so utterly burdened beyond our strength that we despaired of life itself. ⁹Indeed, we felt that we had received the sentence of death. But that was to make us rely not on ourselves but on God who raises the dead. ¹⁰He delivered us from such a deadly peril, and he will deliver us. On him we have set our hope that he will deliver us again. ¹¹You also must help us by prayer, so that many will give thanks on our behalf for the blessing granted us through the prayers of many.

According to these verses, what blessings result from suffering as a Christian? List five or six purposes suffering can serve in our lives.

About six months ago, I joined a workout center that combines weight training and cardio. I've always exercised, but I hadn't spent a lot of time lifting weights, doing push-ups, or running with a weight ball over my head.

When I first began, I was exhausted. I wanted to give up every day. It felt too hard, but I kept going. Slowly, over time, the "suffering" of bearing the weights day after day turned into endurance. I could lift more! And I found myself more hopeful as I saw my strength growing. I knew the hard work was doing something good for my body.

Spiritual growth, as Paul noted, works in a similar way. We don't suffer in vain. God is at work. He builds our endurance, character, and hope as we suffer. Through trials, we understand our need for God and our dependence on Him, and we experience His comfort in new ways.

Being a Christian doesn't immunize us from suffering. In fact, sometimes we experience persecution and trials precisely *because* we believe.

2. Read the following verses and underline what you learn about persecution.

    a. 2 Timothy 3:10–12

    [10]You, however, have followed my teaching, my conduct, my aim in life, my faith, my patience, my love, my steadfastness, [11]my persecutions and sufferings that happened to me at Antioch, at Iconium, and at Lystra— which persecutions I endured; yet from them all the Lord rescued me. [12]Indeed, all who desire to live a godly life in Christ Jesus will be persecuted.

    b. John 15:18–21

    [18]If the world hates you, know that it has hated me before it hated you. [19]If you were of the world, the world would love you as its own; but because you are not of the world, but I chose you out of the world, therefore the world hates you. [20]Remember the word that I said to you: "A servant is not greater than his master." If they persecuted me, they will also persecute you. If they kept my word, they will also keep yours. [21]But all these things they will do to you on account of my name, because they do not know him who sent me.

    According to these verses, what should we expect regarding persecution?

Times of suffering and persecution are difficult. Yet they can also be opportunities. I've heard that jewelers always place diamonds on a black surface so that the light and beauty of the diamond can shine. In the midst of the darkness of our suffering, our faith has the opportunity to shine brightly for all the world to see.

3. Read the following verses and underline the ways we can faithfully respond to suffering.

a. 2 Corinthians 4:15–18

[15]For it is all for your sake, so that as grace extends to more and more people it may increase thanksgiving, to the glory of God.

[16]So we do not lose heart. Though our outer self is wasting away, our inner self is being renewed day by day. [17]For this light momentary affliction is preparing for us an eternal weight of glory beyond all comparison, [18]as we look not to the things that are seen but to the things that are unseen. For the things that are seen are transient, but the things that are unseen are eternal.

b. 1 Peter 2:19–24

[19]For this is a gracious thing, when, mindful of God, one endures sorrows while suffering unjustly. [20]For what credit is it if, when you sin and are beaten for it, you endure? But if when you do good and suffer for it you endure, this is a gracious thing in the sight of God. [21]For to this you have been called, because Christ also suffered for you, leaving you an example, so that you might follow in his steps. [22]He committed no sin, neither was deceit found in his mouth. [23]When he was reviled, he did not revile in return; when he suffered, he did not threaten, but continued entrusting himself to him who judges justly. [24]He himself bore our sins in his body on the tree, that we might die to sin and live to righteousness. By his wounds you have been healed.

c. 1 Peter 4:12–16, 19

[12]Beloved, do not be surprised at the fiery trial when it comes upon you to test you, as though something strange were happening to you. [13]But rejoice insofar as you share Christ's sufferings, that you may also rejoice and be glad when his glory is revealed. [14]If you are insulted for

the name of Christ, you are blessed, because the Spirit of glory and of God rests upon you. [15]But let none of you suffer as a murderer or a thief or an evildoer or as a meddler. [16]Yet if anyone suffers as a Christian, let him not be ashamed, but let him glorify God in that name. . . .

[19]Therefore let those who suffer according to God's will entrust their souls to a faithful Creator while doing good.

According to these verses, what should our attitude be toward the suffering and persecution we endure?

Our commitment to rejoice in God's goodness is most put to the test when we suffer. However, it's also the time when our praise and joy in Christ shine forth in greater radiance, causing the watching world to wonder at our hope.

I recently listened to a podcast with Joni Eareckson Tada, who was paralyzed from the shoulders down in a diving accident that occurred fifty years ago when she was a teenager.[2] On the podcast she described those who suffer in profound ways as "spectacles of glory." They're like the burning bush that prompted Moses to pause in confusion—how could the bush be on fire and yet not be consumed? It was a spectacle of glory, something that made him turn and look in wonder.

Joni explained that Christians who suffer faithfully shine the light of Christ in a way that confounds the watching world. People simply don't understand how someone could be joyful, patient, and kind in the midst of trials. Profound suffering positions us to be spectacles of glory for all the world to see the beauty of Christ in us.

Take some time now to pray. May God strengthen and uphold you in your sufferings so you might walk in a manner worthy of the gospel of Christ—a spectacle of glory, declaring His praise.

DAY 4: APPLICATION

How Does the Text Transform Me?

You may have spent this week wondering, *What exactly does it mean to rejoice in Christ's lordship?* It's a good question. Theologian John Frame explained what it means that God reigns over all things:

> Indeed, his mighty deeds prove him to be no less than King over all the earth. . . . But God does not control only the course of nature and the great events of history. As we have seen, he is also concerned with details. So we find in Scripture that God controls the course of each human life. How could it be otherwise? God controls all natural events in detail, even including apparently random events.[3]

Every story in the Bible points to this truth: God is in charge. He's not a spectator in your life, wondering and watching to see what's going to happen. He reigns over all the details: from the traffic you faced on the way to work to the difficult diagnosis you received at the doctor's office. You are not on plan B (or X, Y, or Z) of your life because of the wrong choices you or someone else made. We often think of our lives as a Choose Your Own Adventure book, but in actuality, God is writing your story, and He knows the way the story goes.

This truth is difficult to understand. It's a mystery. God reigns over all things, and yet we are all responsible for our own actions. None of us can fully understand these two seemingly incompatible truths, but we can believe two things: First, the Scriptures attest to both God's sovereignty and our responsibility as humans. Second, this truth is a great comfort in our lives. The Belgic Confession (written in the sixteenth century) explains,

> This doctrine affords us unspeakable consolation, since we are taught thereby that nothing can befall us by chance, but by the direction of our most gracious and heavenly Father; who watches over us with a paternal care, keeping all creatures so under his power, that not a hair

of our head (for they are all numbered), nor a sparrow, can fall to the ground, without the will of our Father, in whom we do entirely trust; being persuaded, that he so restrains the devil and all our enemies, that without his will and permission, they cannot hurt us.[4]

Take in the good news: the world may seem like a mess, but God is at work. Remember the biblical stories of Joseph, Joshua, Ruth, Esther, and David? Each of their lives took multiple twists and turns. At points, it looked like their circumstances or sin choices had spiraled out of control. People made wrong choices and did them harm. But God was always there, working good from the bad.

The pinnacle of God's redemption was at the cross. The murder of God's Son was the worst thing that ever happened. But it happened precisely because of God's plan: "This Jesus, delivered up according to the definite plan and foreknowledge of God, you crucified and killed by the hands of lawless men" (Acts 2:23). Here we see both God's set plan and humanity's responsibility. It's a mystery, but they work together.

Today we'll be applying these truths to our own lives as we look again at our focus passage in Philippians. Go to the Lord in prayer, asking Him to give you eyes to see the way He is working good for you through your circumstances.

Read **Philippians 1:12–30** on pages 59–60 or in your own Bible.

1. Paul could see that God was using his own difficult circumstances to allow the gospel to spread to many different people. His greatest concern was not for his own comfort but for the gospel to be preached. Often I am too hesitant to tell others about Christ simply because I'm afraid they might reject me or I'll make them uncomfortable. I've never had to worry about them throwing me in jail! What keeps you from telling people about Christ? What shift in perspective could help you overcome that barrier?

2. Have you ever seen God use a difficult circumstance in your life to help others know Christ or encourage them in their faith? If so, describe what happened. If not, describe a time when someone else's response in a trial encouraged you.

3. Paul's attitude while imprisoned was one of inner contentment and joy. He was willing to endure whatever he was called to—shipwrecks, imprisonments, living, or dying—as long as the gospel was being spread and God was glorified.

   a. In what way do difficult circumstances affect your contentment and joy? Give an example to support your answer.

   b. In what areas of your life are you trying to control your circumstances? What would it look like to entrust them to God?

4. Paul's life was centered on Christ. If he lived, he would give his life for the work of Christ. If he died, he would get to depart and be with Christ. What is your life centered on? What are you living for and hoping to gain out of life?

5. What would it look like for you to live a life worthy of the gospel of Christ? How does the belief that God reigns over all the details of life help you do that?

6. What good have you seen come out of suffering in your own life?

A life worthy of the gospel of Christ is fully submitted to God. It's a life of inner abundance, joy, and peace—regardless of outward sufferings. Close your time in prayer today, asking for a heart that trusts God above all else. Use these words from Thomas à Kempis to guide you:

> Lord, you know what is best. May your will decide what shall be done. Give what you will, how much you will, and when you will. Do what you know is best for me, do what pleases you and brings your name most honour. Put me where you will, and deal with me in all things as you please. I am in your hand—turn me backwards and forwards, turn me upside down. Here I am, your servant, ready for anything, for I have no desire to live for myself, but only to live perfectly and worthily for you.[5]

Amen.

DAY 5: DEVOTIONAL

Rejoicing in Christ's Lordship

And we know that in all things God works for the good
of those who love him, who have been called according to
his purpose.

—ROMANS 8:28, NIV

Often I believe that if it were up to me, I'd have joy. If I could be in charge and have free rein to choose what I want my life to look like, surely I'd be able to rejoice. However, there's a significant problem with my thinking. While I may know what's easiest or most comfortable, I don't always know what's best.

If my children could choose, I'm pretty certain they'd pick candy, ice cream, and soda for every meal. It tastes good and makes them happy. So why don't I give them what they want (and what they believe they need)? Because I know these items aren't what's best for them. Their bodies aren't made to run well on only sugar—they need healthy greens and vegetables. They might not want these items (and one of my children might even deem it suffering to eat his broccoli), but healthy food is what's best for them.

Just as my children's understanding is limited, my own perspective of life is restricted. I can't see the whole story. I may know what I like, but I don't necessarily know what's best for the health of my soul.

In this week's study we saw Paul rejoicing in spite of hardship and suffering. He did so because he knew that God was in charge of all the circumstances and events of his life. This knowledge empowered him to endure. Paul understood that God's sovereignty guaranteed He would accomplish all He promised.

So through it all, as he faced the injustice of his chains, Paul rejoiced in the gospel's advancement. When men wrongly preached Christ out of envy and rivalry, Paul rejoiced that Christ was proclaimed. As Paul faced the possibility of death, he rejoiced in the hope of life (his ministry with the Philippians) and death (being with Jesus).

It's important to note that Paul didn't necessarily rejoice in the hardship itself but in God's work in the midst of the trial. In Romans 8, Paul explained that God works all things to the ultimate goal of conforming us into the likeness of Christ.

The bedrock of our rejoicing isn't the goodness of our day but the goodness of our God.

This truth allows us to overflow with praise. We may struggle in our circumstances. We may long for them to change. We may not understand why we face the trials we face.

However, we can hold fast to the precious truth that our tears are never wasted. Every sorrow, trial, and struggle is sifted through the hands of Christ—hands that are nail scarred and full of the deepest love imaginable. What He brings is best. What He has promised He is also *able* to bring about. He is working all things for good. We can rejoice.

Take some time to consider:

1. In what area(s) are you struggling to trust God with your circumstances today?

2. How would you like to live differently? What specific changes is He calling you to make so that you can walk in a manner worthy of the gospel?

Close your time in prayer and praise to our God:

Oh, the depth of the riches and wisdom and knowledge of God! How unsearchable are his judgments and how inscrutable his ways!

"For who has known the mind of the Lord,
    or who has been his counselor?"
"Or who has given a gift to him
    that he might be repaid?"

For from him and through him and to him are all things. To him be glory forever. Amen. (Romans 11:33–36)

The More of Becoming Less

Joy in Humility

Philippians 2:1–11

Humility will make a man quiet and contented in the lowest condition, and it will preserve a man from envying other men's prosperous condition. . . . Humility honors those who are strong in grace, and puts two hands under those who are weak in grace. . . . Humility makes a man richer than other men, and it makes a man judge himself the poorest among men. . . . Humility will make a man have high thoughts of others and low thoughts of himself.

—Thomas Brooks

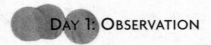

DAY 1: OBSERVATION

What Does the Text Say?

Today I'm going to ask you to do something that you'd probably prefer not to do. It might feel like busy work. You'll be tempted to skip this part. Believe me, I understand. Sometimes the best things we can do are the simplest and the hardest all at the same time.

I'd like for you to pull out your Bible, open it to Philippians, and read it all the way through—all four chapters.

I know you have lots going on in your day and this might feel like one more task that will take too long. But here's why I want you to read it again. When we study the Bible, it's easy to forget the larger story as we focus on the details. We zoom in on the beauty of a verse or a truth, and that's a good thing. But it's also necessary to zoom out and take in the entire view of what we're learning.

If we took a trip to the Grand Canyon, we'd want both views, wouldn't we? We'd want to stand at the top and take in the majesty, as well as hike the canyon to see the layers and beauty from a different perspective.

So today I encourage you to pick up your Bible and read the entire book of Philippians from front to back. I hope you'll be so familiar with the text by the end of our study that when you hear it quoted, you can say to yourself, *Oh, that's from Philippians.*

Before you read, take some time to pray. Put your cares and concerns before the Lord. He loves you. He hears you. He welcomes you.

As you read, look for any themes you see running throughout the entire book. Did anything in particular encourage you today? If so, write it out:

Now that you've read the entire book again, let's focus in on our passage for this week. Read **Philippians 2:1–11** and answer the questions that follow.

¹So if there is any encouragement in Christ, any comfort from love, any participation in the Spirit, any affection and sympathy, ²complete my joy by being of the same mind, having the same love, being in full accord and of one mind. ³Do nothing from selfish ambition or conceit, but in humility count others more significant than yourselves. ⁴Let each of you look not only to his own interests, but also to the interests of others. ⁵Have this mind among yourselves, which is yours in Christ Jesus, ⁶who, though he was in the form of God, did not count equality with God a thing to be grasped, ⁷but emptied himself, by taking the form of a servant, being born in the likeness of men. ⁸And being found in human form, he humbled himself by becoming obedient to the point of death, even death on a cross. ⁹Therefore God has highly exalted him and bestowed on him the name that is above every name, ¹⁰so that at the name of Jesus every knee should bow, in heaven and on earth and under the earth, ¹¹and every tongue confess that Jesus Christ is Lord, to the glory of God the Father.

1. What did Paul say would make his joy complete?

2. What five things formed the basis for unity among the believers at Philippi (verse 1)?

3. How did Paul exhort his readers to relate to one another (verses 3–4)?

4. How does this contrast with Paul's earlier description of how certain believers were behaving? (See Philippians 1:15–17.)

5. Describe the result of Christ's humility, as detailed in verses 9–11.

6. We usually think of the Gospels (Matthew, Mark, Luke, and John) when we want to learn about Jesus, but this passage is a great example of how the whole Bible teaches us about Him. List the things you learn about Jesus from these verses.

This passage in Philippians zooms us in on the beauty of Christ's humility. It's amazing, isn't it? Jesus reigned in heavenly splendor but left it all, humbling Himself from the moment of conception. God became man!

We celebrate this truth every Christmas, but it's difficult to understand. Why would God put on flesh and come to earth? If the Duke and Duchess of Cambridge decided to forego their palaces and make a home in the slums of a foreign country, wouldn't we all be somewhat confused? And their palaces can't compare to the riches Jesus left in heaven—only to be placed in a manger, surrounded by animals.

The gospel of John tells us why He came to earth. It's one of the most famous passages, but consider it again: "For God so loved the world, that he gave his only Son, that whoever believes in him should not perish but have eternal life" (John 3:16).

Jesus humbled Himself because of *love*. He gave His life to give us life. His humility bought our glory. Because He became like us, one day we will become like Him! Amazing love—how can it be?

One of my favorite songs to sing at Christmas is "Thou Who Wast Rich Beyond All Splendor." The opening stanza speaks to the poverty Jesus experienced because of His love for us:

> Thrones for a manger didst surrender,
> Sapphire-paved courts for stable floor.[1]

Jesus emptied Himself of heavenly riches and became poor—all because of love. He came to rescue you and me and promised to prepare a place for us in heaven. Spend some time now considering Christ's humility and asking God to give you a humble heart that looks like His.

Day 2: Interpretation

What Does the Text Mean?

Humility doesn't grow easily. It's a cultivated fruit, while pride springs up like a weed, overtaking everything in its path. We're naturally inclined to focus on self. We want our successes noticed and our faults minimized.

As I watched children playing a few weeks ago, I noticed this natural propensity for both self-congratulation and self-protection. When a good plan came together, one child was quick to claim the glory. "It was my idea!" he shouted, making sure everyone knew his contribution. When a drink spilled, a little girl quickly hid her own culpability, saying, "He knocked my elbow—it's his fault!"

As adults, we tend to be just as quick to see our own successes and another's failures. With self as our focus, it's difficult to consider others more significant than ourselves. It's completely counterintuitive to put someone else's needs before our own. And no one wants to take the blame for another person's mistakes.

Yet that's exactly what Jesus did. He had every reason to receive glory and honor and praise, but He didn't take it. He had done nothing deserving punishment, but He paid the penalty for us all. His humility was a complete reversal of the attitude taken by Adam and Eve. In their pride, they wanted to become like God. In His humility, Jesus became a man.

Today we'll look again at the same passage, seeking to better understand what we observed yesterday. Begin your time with prayer, asking the Lord to give you a clearer understanding of Christ's humility and a willingness to follow His example.

Turn back to page 81 and read **Philippians 2:1–11**.

1. As we saw in week 2, people can be unified in many ways—around a sports team, a nationality, a similar interest, or a variety of other shared

experiences. Paul's basis for unity is union with Christ. According to verse 2, what does it mean to be united to Christ?

2. How does union with Christ lead to like-mindedness in purpose? Why is this important in the church?

3. Does unity in purpose mean that all Christians are to do the exact same things in the exact same ways? Explain your answer.

4. Read **Romans 12:3–8**.

   [3]For by the grace given to me I say to everyone among you not to think of himself more highly than he ought to think, but to think with sober judgment, each according to the measure of faith that God has assigned. [4]For as in one body we have many members, and the members do not all have the same function, [5]so we, though many, are one body in Christ, and individually members one of another. [6]Having gifts that differ according to the grace given to us, let us use them: if prophecy, in proportion to our faith; [7]if service, in our serving; the one who teaches, in his teaching; [8]the one who exhorts, in his exhortation; the one who contributes, in generosity; the one who leads, with zeal; the one who does acts of mercy, with cheerfulness.

   How do these verses help you understand both our unity in Christ and our individuality?

5. Consider the areas of life listed in the chart that follows. In each, what does selfish ambition look like? By contrast, what does humility look like in these interactions?

	Selfish Ambition	Humility
Church Involvement		
Friendship		
Leadership		
Family		
Job/Work		
Community Service		

6. From your own experience and observations, how does selfish ambition tear apart community? How does humility build unity?

7. Thinking back to Acts 16 and what you've learned of Paul so far, in what specific ways did he share in Christ's humility? How did Paul serve others?

8. Why is Christ worthy of the exaltation described in Philippians 2:9–11?

All throughout high school, I played soccer with the same group of girls. We played year round and formed lasting friendships from our shared hours of practice. We had two simple objectives: (1) keep the ball out of our net and (2) put the ball in their net.

To achieve these two items, we had to work together. Our offense might score a ton of goals, but if our defense failed, we'd still lose the game. Our defense might keep the other team from scoring, but if our offense never scored, the best we could hope for would be a tie.

Each individual player needed to practice humility. We had to accept that we needed one another. No one player could do everything on the field. The best of players couldn't win the game without the others doing their job. Each game we had to go out unified and work together or we'd never succeed. There is no room for selfish ambition on a winning team.

Our life as Christ followers also has two objectives: (1) love God and (2) love others. We need one another to accomplish both of these. My love for God will be incomplete without community. And my love for others grows as I experience the fellowship of the Spirit in community.

It's humbling to need someone else. The discomfort of such dependence often leads us to try to be self-sufficient and look out for our own interests. However, we're not created to be Lone Ranger Christians. We're made for community. Our union with Christ unites us to everyone else who's in Christ.

We need one another. Every person matters. The church is incomplete without you, and you are incomplete without the church.

Close your time today praying for humility. Ask the Lord to show you where you're trying to be self-sufficient and pridefully independent. Pride often is revealed in two places: (1) areas where we judge others and (2) situations in which we grow easily upset, hurt, or angry at others.

Where do you see those emotions in your heart today? Are they linked to your pride? In what ways are you looking out for your own interests but missing the needs of those around you? Ask the Lord to give you eyes to see and the humility to change. May He faithfully cultivate a spirit of humility in each of us.

DAY 3: INTERPRETATION

What Does the Text Mean?

Humility doesn't mean we consider ourselves unimportant or unneeded. It's not self-deprecation. Jesus knew His life and mission were of the utmost importance. His humility was shown in His willingness to think of others more than Himself. To paraphrase pastor and theologian Timothy Keller, the essence of gospel-humility is not thinking more of myself or thinking less of myself; it is thinking of myself less.[2]

Christ's entire life was one of humility. From His birth to His death and all the moments in between, He thought of others before Himself. Today we're going to look at some other passages in Scripture that show forth Christ's humility. He's our example to follow.

Open your time in prayer today, asking the Lord to meet you as you study.

1. Read **Luke 2:1–7.**

   ¹In those days a decree went out from Caesar Augustus that all the world should be registered. ²This was the first registration when Quirinius was governor of Syria. ³And all went to be registered, each to his own town. ⁴And Joseph also went up from Galilee, from the town of Nazareth, to Judea, to the city of David, which is called Bethlehem, because he was of the house and lineage of David, ⁵to be registered with Mary, his betrothed, who was with child. ⁶And while they were there, the time came for her to give birth. ⁷And she gave birth to her firstborn son and wrapped him in swaddling cloths and laid him in a manger, because there was no place for them in the inn.

   In what ways were the circumstances of Christ's *birth* humble?

2. Read **Matthew 8:1–4; 9:10–13.**

   ⁸:¹When he came down from the mountain, great crowds followed him. ²And behold, a leper came to him and knelt before him, saying, "Lord, if you will, you can make me clean." ³And Jesus stretched out his hand and touched him, saying, "I will; be clean." And immediately his leprosy was cleansed. ⁴And Jesus said to him, "See that you say nothing to anyone, but go, show yourself to the priest and offer the gift that Moses commanded, for a proof to them." . . .

   ⁹:¹⁰And as Jesus reclined at table in the house, behold, many tax collectors and sinners came and were reclining with Jesus and his disciples. ¹¹And when the Pharisees saw this, they said to his disciples, "Why does your teacher eat with tax collectors and sinners?" ¹²But when he heard it, he said, "Those who are well have no need of a physician, but

those who are sick. ¹³Go and learn what this means, 'I desire mercy, and not sacrifice.' For I came not to call the righteous, but sinners."

How did Jesus demonstrate humility in His *ministry*?

3. Read the following passages. For each, note what you learn regarding humility from Christ's *teaching*.

a. Matthew 20:25–28

²⁵But Jesus called them to him and said, "You know that the rulers of the Gentiles lord it over them, and their great ones exercise authority over them. ²⁶It shall not be so among you. But whoever would be great among you must be your servant, ²⁷and whoever would be first among you must be your slave, ²⁸even as the Son of Man came not to be served but to serve, and to give his life as a ransom for many."

b. John 12:23–26

²³And Jesus answered them, "The hour has come for the Son of Man to be glorified. ²⁴Truly, truly, I say to you, unless a grain of wheat falls into the earth and dies, it remains alone; but if it dies, it bears much fruit. ²⁵Whoever loves his life loses it, and whoever hates his life in this world will keep it for eternal life. ²⁶If anyone serves me, he must follow me; and where I am, there will my servant be also. If anyone serves me, the Father will honor him.

4. Read **John 13:3–5, 12–17.**

³Jesus, knowing that the Father had given all things into his hands, and that he had come from God and was going back to God, ⁴rose from supper. He laid aside his outer garments, and taking a towel, tied it around his waist. ⁵Then he poured water into a basin and began to wash the disciples' feet and to wipe them with the towel that was wrapped around him. . . .

¹²When he had washed their feet and put on his outer garments and resumed his place, he said to them, "Do you understand what I have done to you? ¹³You call me Teacher and Lord, and you are right, for so I am. ¹⁴If I then, your Lord and Teacher, have washed your feet, you also ought to wash one another's feet. ¹⁵For I have given you an example, that you also should do just as I have done to you. ¹⁶Truly, truly, I say to you, a servant is not greater than his master, nor is a messenger greater than the one who sent him. ¹⁷If you know these things, blessed are you if you do them.

How do you see Christ display humility in His *friendships*?

5. Read **John 19:1–6, 16–18.**

¹Then Pilate took Jesus and flogged him. ²And the soldiers twisted together a crown of thorns and put it on his head and arrayed him in a purple robe. ³They came up to him, saying, "Hail, King of the Jews!" and struck him with their hands. ⁴Pilate went out again and said to them, "See, I am bringing him out to you that you may know that I find no guilt in him." ⁵So Jesus came out, wearing the crown of thorns and the purple robe. Pilate said to them, "Behold the man!" ⁶When the chief priests and the officers saw him, they cried out, "Crucify him, crucify him!" Pilate said to them, "Take him yourselves and crucify him, for I find no guilt in him." . . .

[16]So he delivered him over to them to be crucified.

So they took Jesus, [17]and he went out, bearing his own cross, to the place called The Place of a Skull, which in Aramaic is called Golgotha. [18]There they crucified him, and with him two others, one on either side, and Jesus between them.

How do you see Jesus's humility in His *death*?

Jesus's example of humility spanned His entire life. His birth, teaching, friendships, ministry, and death all illuminated both His love for God and His love for others.

In her book *Humble Roots,* Hannah Anderson explained,

> So before we can even begin to answer His call to come to Him, Jesus comes to us. Because we could never sufficiently humble ourselves, Jesus humbles Himself. And by doing so, He became both the model and the means of our own humility.[3]

In our own lives, humility begins when we realize the truth that all we've been given is a gift. There's no such thing as a self-made man or woman. Whatever talents or strengths we may consider "ours"—intelligence, beauty, diligence, creativity— these items are no more our own doing than having brown eyes or blue. Each of us was lovingly and masterfully created. As 1 Corinthians 4:7 questions, "What do you have that you did not receive? If then you received it, why do you boast as if you did not receive it?" Whatever good might come from our lives is the result of God's working in and through us.

Humility is a beautiful thing. Humility allows us to

- pray "Thy will be done" instead of "My will be done"
- consider the needs of others when they may not look out for ours
- obey God's Word even when doing so is costly
- share our faith with gentleness and respect
- see another's need for Christ without judgment

- serve without being noticed
- keep trusting God's goodness when life is hard

Close your time today in prayer, asking the Lord to impress on your heart the humility of Christ. Thank Jesus for how He lived and died for you. May our union with Christ overflow in humility and unity with others.

DAY 4: APPLICATION

How Does the Text Transform Me?

We live in a selfie world. Between Facebook, Twitter, and Instagram, we have so many ways to say "Look at me! Notice me!" It's difficult to live in a way that says "Look to Jesus! Notice Him!"

Jesus noticed the needs of others. He saw their sorrows, their sins, their hurts, their pride, and their joys. Even though He's God and worthy of our notice, He didn't grasp for glory. Instead, He became a servant.

How do we follow in the ways of Jesus? How do we become like Him in His humility? Today we'll return to our passage in Philippians and consider how to apply these truths to our own lives.

Open your time in prayer, asking God to help you to apply His word to your life.

Turn once more to page 81 and read **Philippians 2:1–11**.

1. Paul's exhortation for the Philippians to live in unity is based on five things:
   - encouragement from their union with Christ
   - comfort from Christ's love
   - fellowship with the Spirit
   - affection
   - sympathy

a. How have you experienced encouragement and comfort from Christ's love? Write out three or four examples of how you've been encouraged in your faith and comforted by God's love for you.

b. How does fellowship with the Spirit lead to greater tenderness and compassion toward others?

We all face the temptation to want to be better than others. It is not wrong to work hard at our labors in hopes of doing well, but usually our desire to be *better than* is rooted in our own selfish pursuits. At times our selfish ambition can even take on the appearance of being good. (Think about those in chapter 1 who preached simply to afflict Paul in his imprisonment.) We can serve others with selfish motives, such as hoping that our good deeds will garner attention and approval.

To clarify, it's not a bad thing for our good deeds to be noticed. In fact, Peter said he hoped the Gentiles "may see your good deeds and glorify God" (1 Peter 2:12). The problem comes when we want the glory for ourselves rather than for God.

2. Think through your own motivations—what are you doing out of selfish ambition? Consider your work, your ministry, your mothering, your friendships, and your service. How could you seek to serve in these areas with greater humility?

3. In what areas of life do you tend to consider yourself better than others? In what ways are you most often tempted to judge other people? Be honest with yourself—no one is going to read what you write!

4. First Corinthians 4:7 questions, "For who sees anything different in you? What do you have that you did not receive? If then you received it, why do you boast as if you did not receive it?" Think through the areas you listed in question 3. How does this verse help you shift your perspective and encourage you toward humility in those areas?

5. Consider the people who often frustrate or annoy you. It could be because of their choices and how those choices affect you. It might be because of their attitude or self-focus. What would it look like for you to view these people with humility?

If we're cold, we look for warmth. If we're tired, we seek rest. If we're in pain, we try to find help. If we're hungry we look for food. It's natural to look out for our own interests, and Paul didn't discourage us from taking care of ourselves.

However, he also wanted his readers to look out for the interests of others. Unity with Christ means we're unified with fellow believers. If my sister in Christ has needs, I should be concerned—she's part of my family. If she's hurting, I hurt with her. Christ's love awakens us to love others in new ways.

6. How can you be more aware of the needs of others? Is there someone in your community who is hurting, lonely, or in need? What can you do this week to reach out to that person?

7. In Philippians 1, Paul recommended Timothy and himself as servants of Christ. It takes humility to be willing to serve another person. Whom in your life has God called you to serve? What is your attitude as you serve them?

8. It also takes humility to believe we need a Savior. What in your life points to your need for Jesus today?

Sometimes it's difficult to face what's in our hearts, isn't it? I can be so centered on my plan for the day that I fail to notice the needs of those around me. I can easily think of all the ways my husband can serve me yet fail to consider how I can serve him. I can think of ways I'd like to be praised or noticed, but I overlook those in my life whom I could encourage and praise.

Most of us struggle to consider others' needs before our own. Our natural disposition is to think about ourselves. Yet the more we do so, the more unhappy we become. Self-focus feeds our discontentment.

But there's good news and hope for us all: *the more time we spend with Jesus, the more we become like Him.*

Time spent in God's Word and prayer transforms us. Walking humbly with our God is possible. He gives us new hearts to love others and new eyes to see their needs. Our union with Christ makes unity with others a reality.

Close your time today asking God to cultivate a Christlike humility in your heart. Ask Him to show you areas where you're walking in self-focus and self-sufficiency, and ask Him to change you.

I also encourage you to take some time to pray for others. Who do you know who is hurting or in need? Prayer is a tangible way we can put the needs of others before our own.

DAY 5: DEVOTIONAL

Humility: The Way Up Is the Way Down

> Finally, all of you, have unity of mind, sympathy, brotherly
> love, a tender heart, and a humble mind.
>
> —1 PETER 3:8

A study in Britain of twenty-five hundred children under the age of ten found that, more than anything else, they wanted to be famous.[4] "Good looks" and "being rich" followed as second and third on the list of the "best things in the world."

If our children believe that being famous, good looking, and rich are the keys to joy, we can safely assume they are absorbing these values from the culture surrounding them. As we turn on the television and see numerous reality shows, it doesn't take long to realize we live in a world that encourages self-promotion and self-glorification as a primary means of obtaining happiness.

In contrast to striving for fame and popularity, Jesus willingly cloaked Himself in humanity, taking on the form of a baby. The Creator of the universe became frail enough to be held and rocked by His mother. He invested His life in caring for the "least of these"—the lepers, the poor, the blind, the discouraged, the hopeless, and the vulnerable.

Jesus also willingly served those closest to Him, even though one would betray Him and the other eleven would deny Him. He got down on His knees, took a basin of water, and washed their feet. He not only died for us, He *lived* for thirty-three years outside the glory of heaven. He experienced all the indignity of our humanity and then submitted Himself to death on a cross.

Love led Jesus to the cross, and future joy helped Him endure it. The author of Hebrews explains, "Let us run with endurance the race that is set before us, looking to Jesus, the founder and perfecter of our faith, *who for the joy that was set before him endured the cross,* despising the shame, and is seated at the right hand of the throne of God" (12:1–2).

Paul asked the believers in Philippi to take on the attitude of Christ. He knew their mind-set would form their actions. He hoped for them as parents hope for their children. The joy parents have is made complete when they see their children living a life of service and obedience.

Paul's exhortation to the Philippians to live in humility and unity is not a call to misery and deprivation. It is actually a call to the only life that will satisfy. Our selfish pursuits can't fulfill our longings; they leave us always wanting more. We may gain all this world has to offer and never truly taste joy.

Joy comes by laying down our lives, not by puffing ourselves up.

Our union with Christ allows us to participate in His sufferings and humility, but it also allows us to participate in His joy and exultation. Romans 6:5 promises, "If we have been united with him in a death like his, we shall certainly be united with him in a resurrection like his."

Christ was given the highest place in heaven and the name that is above every name, not because He focused on becoming great, but because He gave His life for others. He emptied Himself, and God exalted Him for all eternity. Following in His path, we can willingly give our lives for others, seeking to serve as we have been served.

Today I encourage you to rejoice in Christ, who lived and died so that you might experience an inner joy independent of outer circumstances. Spend time praying, asking God to give you true joy, which nothing can diminish.

Consider these two things specifically:

1. How can I praise God today?

2. Whom can I serve today?

With Hearts Set Free

Joy in Obedience

Philippians 2:12–30

The more I read the Bible and see the picture of the Christian . . . , the more I understand the nature of sin and life in this world, and what God has done for me in Christ, then the more I shall desire the things of God and hate the other. So I suggest that the best practical step is to read God's word, and to be thoroughly soaked in it.

—Martyn Lloyd-Jones

DAY 1: OBSERVATION

What Does the Text Say?

So far in Philippians we've studied the ways we experience joy in salvation, gospel partnership, Christ's lordship, and humility. These are such different places to find joy than we usually consider. The world sends us in all sorts of directions on the hunt for happiness, but Scripture provides a trusted guide for us to follow. Perhaps we so rarely experience authentic joy because we've been using the wrong treasure map.

This week we're going to explore another unlikely place to find joy: obedience. It's easy to think of obedience in a negative light, isn't it? (Unless, perhaps, you work as a teacher or have children . . . then you probably think of *obey* as a pretty favorable term!) We often see obedience as a constraint on our freedom, being forced to give up something we want.

However, as Paul explained, the Christian life isn't one of shackles but a different sort of freedom than we imagined: "For you were called to freedom, brothers. Only do not use your freedom as an opportunity for the flesh, but through love serve one another" (Galatians 5:13).

We'll observe these themes in our reading for today. Begin with prayer, asking God to open your eyes to understand the Word.

Read **Philippians 2:12–30.**

> ¹²Therefore, my beloved, as you have always obeyed, so now, not only as in my presence but much more in my absence, work out your own salvation with fear and trembling, ¹³for it is God who works in you, both to will and to work for his good pleasure.
>
> ¹⁴Do all things without grumbling or disputing, ¹⁵that you may be blameless and innocent, children of God without blemish in the midst of a crooked and twisted generation, among whom you shine as lights in the world, ¹⁶holding fast to the word of life, so that in the day of Christ I may be proud that I did not run in vain or labor in vain. ¹⁷Even if I am to be poured out as a drink offering upon the sacrificial offering of your

faith, I am glad and rejoice with you all. [18]Likewise you also should be glad and rejoice with me.

[19]I hope in the Lord Jesus to send Timothy to you soon, so that I too may be cheered by news of you. [20]For I have no one like him, who will be genuinely concerned for your welfare. [21]For they all seek their own interests, not those of Jesus Christ. [22]But you know Timothy's proven worth, how as a son with a father he has served with me in the gospel. [23]I hope therefore to send him just as soon as I see how it will go with me, [24]and I trust in the Lord that shortly I myself will come also.

[25]I have thought it necessary to send to you Epaphroditus my brother and fellow worker and fellow soldier, and your messenger and minister to my need, [26]for he has been longing for you all and has been distressed because you heard that he was ill. [27]Indeed he was ill, near to death. But God had mercy on him, and not only on him but on me also, lest I should have sorrow upon sorrow. [28]I am the more eager to send him, therefore, that you may rejoice at seeing him again, and that I may be less anxious. [29]So receive him in the Lord with all joy, and honor such men, [30]for he nearly died for the work of Christ, risking his life to complete what was lacking in your service to me.

1. Whenever we see the word *therefore* in the text, a good question to ask is, what is it *there for*? Look back at the first part of Philippians 2 on page 81. What does the word *therefore* refer to?

2. What did Paul encourage the Philippians to do in verse 12?

3. How were they to obey?

4. By whose power would they obey (verse 13)?

5. In verses 14–16 Paul gave two commands and listed four results he hoped
   to see. List those below.

   a. Two commands:

   b. Four results:

6. How did Paul describe his sacrifices and service? To what imagery was he
   referring? (See Leviticus 4:7.)

7. What was his attitude toward service?

8. List all that you learn about Timothy. What was Paul's hope for him?

9. List all that you learn about Epaphroditus. Why was Paul sending him
   back to the Philippians?

In this part of his letter, Paul's words were both prescriptive and descriptive. He explained to the Philippians how they should live (prescriptive), and then he shared with them about Timothy and Epaphroditus—two men who exemplified service to others (descriptive). He told them and he showed them what obedience involves.

Today, is there an area of life where you're struggling to obey? Does it feel impossible to do the right thing? Are you having difficulty forgiving or being kind to a certain person? Is there someone who needs your help, but you struggle to serve him or her? Are you weighed down by past failures and wonder if you can ever live differently?

The beautiful truth of the gospel is that, by Christ's power, we're able to increasingly walk in God's ways. In Christ we're freed from sin's penalty and its power. As Paul rejoiced, "Thanks be to God, that you who were once slaves of sin have become obedient from the heart to the standard of teaching to which you were committed" (Romans 6:17).

We're bound by sin no longer. By the Spirit's power, we can be patient, kind, loving, and self-controlled. We may not live perfectly, but we can live powerfully—Jesus lives in us! As we live in obedience to God, even when it's difficult, we experience a new freedom and joy. We become a blessing to others.

Take some time to pray. Maybe you're struggling with anger or impatience, lust or greed. Perhaps you're envious or discontent. Whatever it might be, go to the Lord.

Speaking of Jesus as our high priest, Hebrews 4:15–16 exhorts us,

> For we do not have a high priest who is unable to sympathize with our
> weaknesses, but one who in every respect has been tempted as we are,
> yet without sin. Let us then with confidence draw near to the throne
> of grace, that we may receive mercy and find grace to help in time of
> need.

Approach the throne with confidence, not because of who you are, but because of who Jesus is—sympathetic, merciful, and gracious. You needn't fear condemnation; simply receive His mercy. His grace changes us and gives us strength to obey even in difficult circumstances. Ask and you will receive. Seek and you will find.

DAY 2: INTERPRETATION

What Does the Text Mean?

Today we're going to spend some time digging deeper and looking at Philippians 2:12–13 specifically.

> ¹²Therefore, my beloved, as you have always obeyed, so now, not only
> as in my presence but much more in my absence, work out your own
> salvation with fear and trembling, ¹³for it is God who works in you,
> both to will and to work for his good pleasure.

I want us to think through two questions:

1. What does it mean to fear the Lord?
2. How is a person saved—by his or her own works or by God's work?

In order to think through those questions, we'll look at other Bible passages to help us understand the fear of the Lord and how we're saved. When verses seem confusing or unclear, the best way to understand them more fully is to look at other passages. We let Scripture interpret Scripture. That way, we'll gain a deeper understanding of what Paul was saying to the Philippians.

Begin your time with prayer, asking God to help you understand what it means to fear the Lord (and what it doesn't mean!) and the nature of salvation.

1. Read the following passages, and in the space provided after the last one, note what truth about God each reveals and how we should respond. If you prefer, you can also just underline these truths as you see them in the passage.

   a. Jeremiah 5:22–25

> ²²Do you not fear me? declares the LORD.
>   Do you not tremble before me?
> I placed the sand as the boundary for the sea,
>   a perpetual barrier that it cannot pass;

though the waves toss, they cannot prevail;

    though they roar, they cannot pass over it.

²³But this people has a stubborn and rebellious heart;

    they have turned aside and gone away.

²⁴They do not say in their hearts,

    "Let us fear the LORD our God,

who gives the rain in its season,

    the autumn rain and the spring rain,

and keeps for us

    the weeks appointed for the harvest."

²⁵Your iniquities have turned these away,

    and your sins have kept good from you.

b. Psalm 119:117–120

¹¹⁷Hold me up, that I may be safe

    and have regard for your statutes continually!

¹¹⁸You spurn all who go astray from your statutes,

    for their cunning is in vain.

¹¹⁹All the wicked of the earth you discard like dross,

    therefore I love your testimonies.

¹²⁰My flesh trembles for fear of you,

    and I am afraid of your judgments.

c. Luke 8:25

He said to them, "Where is your faith?" And they were afraid, and they marveled, saying to one another, "Who then is this, that he commands even winds and water, and they obey him?"

d. Luke 12:4–5

⁴I tell you, my friends, do not fear those who kill the body, and after that have nothing more that they can do. ⁵But I will warn you whom

to fear: fear him who, after he has killed, has authority to cast into hell.
Yes, I tell you, fear him!

e. 1 Peter 1:17–19

¹⁷And if you call on him as Father who judges impartially according to
each one's deeds, conduct yourselves with fear throughout the time of
your exile, ¹⁸knowing that you were ransomed from the futile ways
inherited from your forefathers, not with perishable things such as silver
or gold, ¹⁹but with the precious blood of Christ, like that of a lamb
without blemish or spot.

What is true about God?
*God is Creator
(Jeremiah 5:22–23).*

How should we respond?
*We should rightly fear God and trust
Him for provision (Jeremiah 5:24).*

2. Read the following verses as you consider these questions: What does it
    look like to fear God? How does a person who fears God live?

    a. Proverbs 8:13

The fear of the LORD is hatred of evil.

    b. Proverbs 2:1–6

¹My son, if you receive my words
    and treasure up my commandments with you,
²making your ear attentive to wisdom
    and inclining your heart to understanding;
³yes, if you call out for insight

and raise your voice for understanding,
⁴if you seek it like silver
   and search for it as for hidden treasures,
⁵then you will understand the fear of the LORD
   and find the knowledge of God.
⁶For the LORD gives wisdom;
   from his mouth come knowledge and understanding.

c. Ecclesiastes 12:13

The end of the matter; all has been heard. Fear God and keep his commandments, for this is the whole duty of man.

d. Exodus 1:15–21

¹⁵Then the king of Egypt said to the Hebrew midwives, one of whom was named Shiphrah and the other Puah, ¹⁶"When you serve as midwife to the Hebrew women and see them on the birthstool, if it is a son, you shall kill him, but if it is a daughter, she shall live." ¹⁷But the midwives feared God and did not do as the king of Egypt commanded them, but let the male children live. ¹⁸So the king of Egypt called the midwives and said to them, "Why have you done this, and let the male children live?" ¹⁹The midwives said to Pharaoh, "Because the Hebrew women are not like the Egyptian women, for they are vigorous and give birth before the midwife comes to them." ²⁰So God dealt well with the midwives. And the people multiplied and grew very strong. ²¹And because the midwives feared God, he gave them families.

e. 2 Corinthians 5:9–10

⁹So whether we are at home or away, we make it our aim to please him. ¹⁰For we must all appear before the judgment seat of Christ, so that each one may receive what is due for what he has done in the body, whether good or evil.

Based on what you just read, list at least four ways a fear of God is shown in our actions.

3. Read the following verses and underline, circle, or highlight the blessings of fearing God.

   a. Proverbs 9:10

   The fear of the LORD is the beginning of wisdom,
      and the knowledge of the Holy One is insight.

   b. Proverbs 19:23

   The fear of the LORD leads to life,
      and whoever has it rests satisfied;
      he will not be visited by harm.

   c. Proverbs 16:6

   By steadfast love and faithfulness iniquity is atoned for,
      and by the fear of the LORD one turns away from evil.

   d. Proverbs 29:25

   The fear of man lays a snare,
      but whoever trusts in the LORD is safe.

4. Read **Ecclesiastes 8:13**.

   But it will not be well with the wicked, neither will he prolong his days
   like a shadow, because he does not fear before God.

What happens to those who do not fear God?

5. How is a person saved? Read these three passages and answer the questions that follow.

Therefore do not be ashamed of the testimony about our Lord, nor of me his prisoner, but share in suffering for the gospel by the power of God, who saved us and called us to a holy calling, not because of our works but because of his own purpose and grace, which he gave us in Christ Jesus before the ages began. (2 Timothy 1:8–9)

For by grace you have been saved through faith. And this is not your own doing; it is the gift of God, not a result of works, so that no one may boast. For we are his workmanship, created in Christ Jesus for good works, which God prepared beforehand, that we should walk in them. (Ephesians 2:8–10)

Because, if you confess with your mouth that Jesus is Lord and believe in your heart that God raised him from the dead, you will be saved. For with the heart one believes and is justified, and with the mouth one confesses and is saved. For the Scripture says, "Everyone who believes in him will not be put to shame." For there is no distinction between Jew and Greek; for the same Lord is Lord of all, bestowing his riches on all who call on him. For "everyone who calls on the name of the Lord will be saved." (Romans 10:9–13)

a. What role does God play in salvation?

b. What is our role in salvation?

c. What role do our works have in salvation?

6. Based on all the verses you've read today, how would you explain to someone what it means to work out your salvation with fear and trembling?

You've looked at many verses today, and I hope they've helped provide greater clarity on Philippians 2:12–13. In this passage Paul was *not* telling the Philippians how to earn salvation. He was explaining how salvation is lived out in those who are *already* saved.

Our salvation is fully a gift of God. You and I don't bring anything to this party. We get to come freely, without labor and without cost.

And it's a gift that keeps on giving. We're saved not only from judgment in the future but also from the power of sin in the present. We're saved not *by* our good works but *for* good works (Ephesians 2:10).

One sign of this heart change is that we rightly fear God. It's not a cowering fear, one that causes us to run away from God. It's an awe-filled reverence that causes us to live in new ways. Like a caterpillar in the process of becoming a beautiful butterfly, we begin to change. We seek to honor God in everything we do and say and think. This transformation doesn't happen all at once, but gradually our lives begin to look more and more like Jesus.

The burden of the law is lifted. It no longer weighs us down in condemnation. Rather, the law acts as a guide, showing us what life by the Spirit looks like. And because Jesus is changing us, we can rejoice with the psalmist, "I run in the path of your commands, for you have set my heart free" (Psalm 119:32, NIV).

Our hearts are free to run in the path of His commands—isn't that imagery beautiful? Sin doesn't have the power to enslave us any longer. Rejoice in the good news today. Spend some time thanking God for setting your heart free to live in new ways. Pray and ask Him to continue to do His work in those places where it is difficult for you to obey. And ask Him for joyful obedience. What seems impossible to us is possible with God.

DAY 3: INTERPRETATION

What Does the Text Mean?

In his infamous song "Only the Good Die Young," Billy Joel proudly sings,

> I'd rather laugh with the sinners than cry with the saints
> Sinners are much more fun.

It's a catchy and lighthearted song, and we can easily find ourselves believing the message. We worry that if we obey God, if we follow after Him in all His ways, our lives will become bland and boring. The sinners have all the fun, right?

The longer I live, the more I'm convinced of the exact opposite. I've found so much peace and joy by following God's Word, and I've experienced so much pain and regret in my sinful choices. Gossip initially tastes sweet but turns sour. Anger overflows in arguing and complaining. Envy makes enemies of everyone. Pride prevents kindness. Selfishness alienates others. There's not a lot of joy in sin—just pain, heartache, and brokenness. It may appear free and fun, but in the end it always costs too much.

Today we'll look again at the passage in Philippians that opened our week's study, seeking to grasp the meaning of these verses. Open your time by asking the Lord to give you insight.

Read **Philippians 2:12–30** on pages 100–101.

1. Why did Paul want the Philippians to obey?

2. Based on these verses and what we studied yesterday, how would you summarize what it means to fear the Lord?

3. How is our obedience rooted in God's work? Can we please God apart from Jesus? Explain your answer.

4. In what ways do grumbling and disputing bring disunity in a community?

5. How does humility stifle grumbling and disputing? How does pride lead to grumbling and disputing?

6. Why would being blameless and pure allow Paul's readers to shine like stars in a crooked and twisted generation? When do stars shine the brightest?

7. What are some of the benefits we receive from light? List two or three ways it makes a difference in how we function.

8. How does shining our spiritual light help others?

9. What do you think is the difference between being *glad,* as Paul described himself in verses 17 and 18, and being *happy*?

10. In what ways do you see familial unity in Paul's discussion of both Timothy and Epaphroditus?

11. How did Paul's relationship with Timothy, Epaphroditus, and the Philippians demonstrate that he practiced the very thing he preached to them? How did he show humility, selflessness, unity, a lack of grumbling and disputing, and joy?

As God works within us, our lives shine brightly. Think of all the practical benefits of light: It helps us see where we are going. It provides warmth. It helps things to grow. It helps us understand the world around us.

As we obey God, doing all things without grumbling and disputing, we shine before the world. We display what it looks like to follow God. We offer the warmth of God's goodness. We help others grow in their understanding of God. As the famous Welsh minister Dr. Martyn Lloyd-Jones noted,

> You and I are to be people like that; something of the radiance of God is to be on our face and in the whole of our personality, so that, of necessity, we stand out in society as lights in the world, as luminaries in the heavens.[1]

Standing out and being different isn't always comfortable. Some people prefer to live in the darkness, and they feel exposed by Christians who live in the light.

People may mock us, misunderstand us, or say unkind words about our choices. We cannot control how others respond. Our goal is simply to please God in all things:

> Keep your conduct among the Gentiles honorable, so that when they
> speak against you as evildoers, they may see your good deeds and glorify
> God on the day of visitation. (1 Peter 2:12)

Close your time today in prayer, asking the Lord to shine through your life. May others see your good deeds and glorify God.

DAY 4: APPLICATION

How Does the Text Transform Me?

When we lived in Cambridge, England, our children loved taking the train to London. They spent the hour-long trip pointing out all the sheep and cows in the countryside. The ride was smooth, relaxing, and peaceful as we chugged along the tracks.

But imagine if the train had come off its tracks. No longer would we have been calmly counting sheep; we would have been jolted around, hanging on for dear life.

Typically, trains are an enjoyable way to travel. But when they come off their tracks, not only do they not run smoothly, but eventually they come to a crashing halt.

Somewhat like trains, we're designed to run along a certain path, to live in obedience to God's Word. When we get off track, our lives don't run smoothly. While it might look like freedom to go our own way, it's actually just the opposite. We live *more* freely when we live as God intended us to live. His commands are the tracks He's provided for us to travel along smoothly. He's not trying to harm us or keep something from us—He's showing us the best way to live.

This doesn't mean obedience is always easy. Sometimes we don't understand why God's ways are better. Sometimes we're tempted to grumble and complain. Today we'll revisit Philippians 2:12–30, seeking to apply it to our own lives. Pray and ask God to give you eyes to see the goodness of His Word and fill you with the desire to obey Him in all things.

Read **Philippians 2:12–30** on pages 100–101 or in your own Bible.

1. When we trust the Lord with our lives and believe in His goodness, we're willing to obey Him. Just as it took humility for Jesus to obey the Father to the point of death, it takes humility for us to turn from our sins and walk in obedience to God's ways.

   a. How is disobedience a form of pride?

   b. We all have certain sin struggles that come up repeatedly in our lives. What is one particular area in which you find yourself prone to disobedience? What are you afraid of losing if you obey God?

Martyn Lloyd-Jones offered insight into what it means to work out our salvation with fear and trembling:

> He does not mean that we must do it in fear of losing our salvation.
> You will find that in the New Testament these words never carry that implication. . . . Neither is it a kind of craven fear, one of self-torment. It means humility and a holy reverence, or, if you like, a holy vigilance and circumspection. It means that as I work out my salvation, I should realise the tremendous seriousness of what I am doing.[2]

This is a helpful explanation of the passage we've been studying this week. As Christians we aren't meant to live in fearful expectation of condemnation but in joyful remembrance of salvation. We want to please God and follow His commands because we know obedience is important work. It doesn't save us, but it shows forth the glory of God's work within us.

2. Do you fear God in a way that causes you to hide from Him? What's the difference between that and a loving reverence for God? How would it change your relationship with God if you viewed Him as a loving Father?

3. Do you ever neglect your faith or take your salvation for granted rather than working out your salvation with fear and trembling? Explain your answer.

4. Which of God's commands do you tend to resist, either because you view them as unnecessary or too difficult? What might happen if you obeyed?

5. As you consider the past year or two, where do you see God at work in your life? How do you see Him working to change you and grow your faith?

6. As you look back on your life, can you think of a specific time when you're thankful you obeyed God's Word? What was the result? Can you think of a time when you disobeyed? What was the outcome of your disobedience?

7. Think through your average day. When do you find yourself grumbling? Disputing? How would a greater humility or selflessness change your response?

8. Consider the various people in your life. Do any in particular shine with a joy and radiance that is different? What makes them stand out to you?

Paul spoke of both Timothy and Epaphroditus with tenderness, as though he were speaking of his family. They serve as examples of what it looks like to live in true community. It's different from the "I'll scratch your back if you'll scratch mine" ways of the world. It's servant hearted. It's sacrificial. It's other centered. It's risky to love this way, but it can bring great joy.

9. In what ways have you experienced care from others who are not part of your physical family?

10. In what ways have you given care to others who are not part of your physical family? Who could you actively care for and love today as you would a family member?

11. Think of someone you know who is laboring diligently for the work of Christ. What are some ways you can encourage, honor, or support this person?

It's easy for us to go about our days without giving much thought to the spiritual dangers that surround us. We're like children who are often unaware of physical dangers. When my children were little, they'd run into the street without a passing thought about the danger of cars. They'd jump in the deep end of the pool even though they were unable to swim. They'd eat all the candy they could get their hands on. They didn't understand the dangers around them or what was best for them. Because I love them, I gave them rules to keep them safe.

God is like a parent to us and much wiser. He created us. He knows how we work best. He understands the dangers we cannot see. We're limited in our understanding. What seems best isn't always best. Many times our inclinations are wrong. This sober understanding of ourselves causes us to ask, *How do I know which way to go in this confusing world? How do I know if I'm following God's ways or my ways?*

Psalm 119:105 says of God, "Your word is a lamp to my feet and a light to my path." The Bible illuminates our path, showing us which way to go. We may not always understand, but the longer we follow Jesus, the more we realize His plan is good and His ways are right. We can trust Him.

Close your time in prayer, asking God for the strength to obey in all things without grumbling or disputing. Ask that by His grace you would be enabled to work out your salvation, knowing that it is God who is at work within you.

DAY 5: DEVOTIONAL

Joyful Obedience

Open my eyes, that I may behold
wondrous things out of your law.

—PSALM 119:18

Years ago I was driving home after a trip to visit my parents. The highway route was familiar, so I traveled along listening to music, letting my mind wander. About an hour into my trip, I noticed a truck was following me. When I switched lanes, he'd switch lanes. If I slowed down to let him pass, he'd slow down as well. If I sped up, he did the same. It began to unnerve and unsettle me. *Why is he following me?* I wondered.

I tried to act as if I didn't notice him, but I was keenly aware of his presence. It bothered me. It weighed on me. It was raining and getting darker with each minute. I was no longer carefree but burdened.

As I drove, I gradually realized that my eyes felt strained. I'd been concentrating so hard I hadn't noticed how dark it had become. All of a sudden it hit me: my lights weren't on! In the midst of the dark and rain, I'd been driving along the highway with no light to guide me.

As soon I turned them on, the truck that had been tracking with me sped up and went on his way. I now understood why he'd been following me. He'd been seeking to help and guide me because my lights weren't on. While I felt burdened and bothered by his presence, he'd actually been protecting me. He wanted good for me, not harm. My misunderstanding of the situation caused me to fear.

It's easy to view God in the same way, isn't it? We think He's after us, following us. The law can seem to be a burden as well, always declaring, "Not good enough!" And the law does help us to understand the ways we've failed and show us our need for Jesus. But it serves an additional purpose in the life of a believer.

Once we come to Christ (and the lights turn on in our hearts), we're free from the law's condemnation. We now understand God's Word in a new way. What once seemed to threaten us now becomes our guide, comfort, and blessing.

If we misunderstand the purpose of obedience in the life of a Christian, we'll fear the wrong things in the wrong ways. Our misplaced fear will rob us of freedom and joy.

Our Reason to Obey

We don't obey in order to gain salvation. None of us are able to do that. Paul commanded the Philippians to *work out their salvation*. They were to *work out* what God had already *worked in* them. The power of the Holy Spirit in our lives makes our obedience possible.

The understanding that God is working in us spurs us on toward obedience. He has set our hearts free to run in the path of His commands (Psalm 119:32, NIV). The fruit of His work overflows in love, joy, peace, patience, kindness, goodness, faithfulness, gentleness, and self-control (Galatians 5:22–23).

Our Attitude as We Obey

Jesus displayed the full extent of God's love. For our sakes, Christ became "obedient to the point of death, even death on a cross" (Philippians 2:8). In response, our attitude toward God is one of humble reverence and loving affection that overflows in a desire to obey. We work with fear and trembling not because we fear punishment but because we are overcome with awe and amazement at the God of our salvation. We want to please Him in every way, with cheerful and eager hearts. Complacency has no place in our lives. God is worthy and God is at work; therefore, we put our best efforts toward obedience.

The Blessings of Obedience

Our obedience results in blessing; we shine like stars in the universe. As Jesus works through His people, we share His goodness with others. In the midst of the darkness of depravity, light shines into the prevailing emptiness.

Do you remember the story Jesus told of the wise man who built his house on the rock and the foolish man who built his house on the sand? The storm came to both houses, but only one stood firm. Jesus told His disciples, "Everyone then who hears these words of mine *and does them* will be like a wise man who built his house on the rock" (Matthew 7:24). By following God's ways, we build our lives on the only rock that is strong and stable enough to support us. The life of a believer shines not because we are able to avoid painful trials but because our foundation is secure.

What are you building your life on? What's your foundation? Is it secure or sandy? Take some time to consider these two questions:

1. What would "work[ing] out your own salvation with fear and trembling" look like specifically for you today?

2. Are you holding fast to God's Word? What guides your choices, thoughts, and actions?

Our joy comes not as we go our own way but as we follow Jesus. I urge you to take seriously your salvation—work it out with fear and trembling—*for God is at work in you.* The greater the delight you experience in His Word, the greater the delight you'll experience in life.

A Friend Like No Other

Joy in Knowing Christ

Philippians 3:1–11

Knowing God is a matter of *personal involvement,* in mind, will, and feeling. It would not, indeed, be a fully personal relationship otherwise. To get to know another person, you have to commit yourself to his company and interests, and be ready to identify yourself with his concerns. Without this, your relationship with him can only be superficial and flavourless.

—J. I. Packer

DAY 1: OBSERVATION

What Does the Text Say?

As my husband and I chatted this morning before work, he recounted a story that happened years ago when he was leading a youth trip in Mexico. A couple on the beach whom he'd never met before found out he was a minister and asked if he would do a vow renewal service for them right then and there. Somewhat reluctantly he agreed, and it ended up being extremely awkward. We laughed together as he recounted all the details of the story.

We've been married twenty years, yet I'd never before heard that story. Even though I think I know him pretty well (as well as anyone else), I'm still discovering things about him.

If we're paying attention, we're always learning new things about the people in our lives. We want to know them more because we love them.

This week we're going to consider the most important relationship in our lives. We build a friendship with Jesus just as we build a friendship with anyone else. We spend time with Him. We learn about Him through His words, and we talk to Him through prayer.

Knowing Jesus is not a one-time event but a lifelong pursuit. We'll be learning new things about Him for all eternity. Everything we learn affects how we view the world around us. Knowing Jesus changes how we think, how we live, and how we understand ourselves. There's no better person to know.

Today, begin by pulling out your Bible and reading the entire book of Philippians again. I promise you'll see things this time that you missed last time! Read it all the way through, and today focus on the concept of joy. Underline, highlight, or mark in some way each time you notice Paul using any form of the words *joy* or *rejoice*.

Then spend some time in prayer, asking God to help you understand His Word and know Him more and more as you read it.

This week we'll be studying **Philippians 3:1–11**. Take a moment to reread this passage and answer the questions that follow.

[1]Finally, my brothers, rejoice in the Lord. To write the same things to you is no trouble to me and is safe for you.

[2]Look out for the dogs, look out for the evildoers, look out for those who mutilate the flesh. [3]For we are the circumcision, who worship by the Spirit of God and glory in Christ Jesus and put no confidence in the flesh—[4]though I myself have reason for confidence in the flesh also. If anyone else thinks he has reason for confidence in the flesh, I have more: [5]circumcised on the eighth day, of the people of Israel, of the tribe of Benjamin, a Hebrew of Hebrews; as to the law, a Pharisee; [6]as to zeal, a persecutor of the church; as to righteousness under the law, blameless. [7]But whatever gain I had, I counted as loss for the sake of Christ. [8]Indeed, I count everything as loss because of the surpassing worth of knowing Christ Jesus my Lord. For his sake I have suffered the loss of all things and count them as rubbish, in order that I may gain Christ [9]and be found in him, not having a righteousness of my own that comes from the law, but that which comes through faith in Christ, the righteousness from God that depends on faith—[10]that I may know him and the power of his resurrection, and may share his sufferings, becoming like him in his death, [11]that by any means possible I may attain the resurrection from the dead.

1. What did Paul command in verse 1? Why?

2. Whom did he tell the Philippians to watch out for?

3. Whom did Paul identify as "the circumcision"? (That term may be confusing or unfamiliar, so tomorrow we'll look further at what Paul meant by it.) List three characteristics of the true circumcision.

4. List all the reasons Paul might have placed confidence in his flesh.

5. What value did he place on those items once he chose to follow Jesus?

6. Where did Paul find his righteousness?

7. What did Paul desire? List four or five things he mentioned.

Have you ever had a friend you just couldn't wait to get more time with, someone you longed to know better? That's how Paul felt about Jesus. He knew Jesus, but he wanted to know Him more.

Do you want to know Jesus more? Do you long to know Him better? Or do you feel like Jesus is distant and far away? Or perhaps you believe you already know Him pretty well and there's not much to learn?

How would you describe your affections: Do you love Jesus? Is He wonderful to you? Do you delight in what you learn about Him? Take a few minutes to pause and consider these questions. You don't need to write anything down. Just reflect for a moment.

Our affections matter. The more we know Jesus, the more we love Him, and the more we love Him, the more we want to know Him. If you're feeling cold and distant this morning, pray the Lord will warm your affections. If you desire to know Jesus more, pray the Lord will meet you in that longing. Close your time in prayer, and go to Jesus with all that's on your heart this morning. Speak to Him as you would a friend.

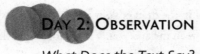

DAY 2: OBSERVATION

What Does the Text Say?

When we lived overseas in Scotland, I taught math at a local high school. One morning I asked my students what I thought was a relatively easy question. I put the equation $Z + 4 = 6$ on the board and asked, "What must Z equal to make this equation work?"

My students looked at me with confusion on their faces. Finally one of them asked, "Do you mean *zed*?" Now it was my turn to be confused. I wondered to myself, *What on earth are they talking about? This is such an easy problem. If they don't get this, I'm not sure what to do with them!*

I said, "No, I'm asking what Z must be in this equation." Again they asked about the word *zed*. We went round and round until I finally understood. While Americans say "X, Y, Z [zee]," the British say "X, Y, Z [zed]." It was difficult for them to answer my question because they didn't understand what I was asking!

All cultures (even similar ones) have differences that can lead to confusion. Just as I was unaware of the differences between the British and American alphabet, we can be unaware of certain significant cultural differences as we read the Bible. It's clear from the passage we read yesterday that Paul was upset, but it may be difficult for us to understand why.

This morning we'll take some time to learn about circumcision so that we'll be better able to understand Paul's concern. By looking at both Old Testament and New Testament passages on this topic, we'll gain helpful insights into the reason for Paul's stern warning to the Philippians.

Open your time with prayer, asking God to meet you today.

Read **Genesis 17:9–14.**

> ⁹And God said to Abraham, "As for you, you shall keep my covenant, you and your offspring after you throughout their generations. ¹⁰This is my covenant, which you shall keep, between me and you and your offspring after you: Every male among you shall be circumcised. ¹¹You

shall be circumcised in the flesh of your foreskins, and it shall be a sign of the covenant between me and you. [12]He who is eight days old among you shall be circumcised. Every male throughout your generations, whether born in your house or bought with your money from any foreigner who is not of your offspring, [13]both he who is born in your house and he who is bought with your money, shall surely be circumcised. So shall my covenant be in your flesh an everlasting covenant. [14]Any uncircumcised male who is not circumcised in the flesh of his foreskin shall be cut off from his people; he has broken my covenant."

1. With whom did God establish the covenant of circumcision?

2. Why did God want them to be circumcised?

3. When was it to be done? To whom?

4. What was the consequence of failure to circumcise?

Circumcision was an integral part of belonging to the nation of Israel. While it was an outward physical sign, it represented an important inner spiritual reality. The following three passages give insight into the greater hope of a circumcised heart.

5. Read **Deuteronomy 10:15–21.**

[15]Yet the LORD set his heart in love on your fathers and chose their offspring after them, you above all peoples, as you are this day. [16]Cir-

cumcise therefore the foreskin of your heart, and be no longer stubborn. [17]For the LORD your God is God of gods and Lord of lords, the great, the mighty, and the awesome God, who is not partial and takes no bribe. [18]He executes justice for the fatherless and the widow, and loves the sojourner, giving him food and clothing. [19]Love the sojourner, therefore, for you were sojourners in the land of Egypt. [20]You shall fear the LORD your God. You shall serve him and hold fast to him, and by his name you shall swear. [21]He is your praise. He is your God, who has done for you these great and terrifying things that your eyes have seen.

a. What type of circumcision is mentioned here?

b. How is it different from the circumcision described in Genesis 17? What does it involve?

c. List the identifying traits of those who are circumcised in heart, according to this passage.

6. Read **Deuteronomy 30:6–8.**

[6]And the LORD your God will circumcise your heart and the heart of your offspring, so that you will love the LORD your God with all your heart and with all your soul, that you may live. [7]And the LORD your God will put all these curses on your foes and enemies who persecuted you. [8]And you shall again obey the voice of the LORD and keep all his commandments that I command you today.

a. What promise about circumcision is given in this passage?

b. According to these verses, how does it look to be circumcised in heart?

The outward sign of circumcision was of vital importance to the Jewish nation. This led to confusion and controversy in the early church, as both Jews and Gentiles came to faith. The debate over circumcision in the early church is described in Acts.

7. Read **Acts 15:1, 6–11.**

> ¹But some men came down from Judea and were teaching the brothers, "Unless you are circumcised according to the custom of Moses, you cannot be saved." . . .
>
> ⁶The apostles and the elders were gathered together to consider this matter. ⁷And after there had been much debate, Peter stood up and said to them, "Brothers, you know that in the early days God made a choice among you, that by my mouth the Gentiles should hear the word of the gospel and believe. ⁸And God, who knows the heart, bore witness to them, by giving them the Holy Spirit just as he did to us, ⁹and he made no distinction between us and them, having cleansed their hearts by faith. ¹⁰Now, therefore, why are you putting God to the test by placing a yoke on the neck of the disciples that neither our fathers nor we have been able to bear? ¹¹But we believe that we will be saved through the grace of the Lord Jesus, just as they will."

a. What was the nature of the debate between the two groups?

b. What was the resolution?

8. The writers of the New Testament explained the deeper meaning of circumcision to their congregations. Read each of the following New Testament passages and record what you learn from each about true circumcision.

a. Romans 2:28–29

[28]For no one is a Jew who is merely one outwardly, nor is circumcision outward and physical. [29]But a Jew is one inwardly, and circumcision is a matter of the heart, by the Spirit, not by the letter. His praise is not from man but from God.

b. Colossians 2:11–14

[11]In him also you were circumcised with a circumcision made without hands, by putting off the body of the flesh, by the circumcision of Christ, [12]having been buried with him in baptism, in which you were also raised with him through faith in the powerful working of God, who raised him from the dead. [13]And you, who were dead in your trespasses and the uncircumcision of your flesh, God made alive together with him, having forgiven us all our trespasses, [14]by canceling the record of debt that stood against us with its legal demands. This he set aside, nailing it to the cross.

c. Galatians 6:12–16

¹²It is those who want to make a good showing in the flesh who would force you to be circumcised, and only in order that they may not be persecuted for the cross of Christ. ¹³For even those who are circumcised do not themselves keep the law, but they desire to have you circumcised that they may boast in your flesh. ¹⁴But far be it from me to boast except in the cross of our Lord Jesus Christ, by which the world has been crucified to me, and I to the world. ¹⁵For neither circumcision counts for anything, nor uncircumcision, but a new creation. ¹⁶And as for all who walk by this rule, peace and mercy be upon them, and upon the Israel of God.

God wants our affections. The outward signs of faith are important, but true renewal starts inside and works its way out. In Christ, we're given new hearts, ones that love God and long to walk in His ways. Our obedience is not a way to earn God's favor but the natural overflow of God's work in our hearts.

God wants more from you than obedience. Go to Him now, asking for a circumcised heart that overflows with an ever-deepening love for Jesus.

Day 3: Interpretation

What Does the Text Mean?

Look out! That's how we alert others to danger, isn't it? We want to warn them something's coming their way that has the power to hurt them—it might be a ball heading straight for them, a car speeding down the street, or a person they should avoid.

After beginning this section with a reminder to "rejoice in the Lord," Paul used the phrase "look out" three times. He was concerned for the welfare of his readers. While it may seem that he switched topics abruptly, the warnings he gave were directly linked to his reminder to rejoice.

It's a bit like when I drop my children off at the pool for the day. I tell them,

"Have fun!" and then I give them a list of motherly reminders: "Make sure you reapply sunscreen. Listen to the lifeguards. Spend some time in the shade. Drink lots of water." My warnings go hand in hand with my desire for them to have a good day. I know sunburn or heat exhaustion will prevent them from having fun, so I warn them, "Look out!"

Paul's warnings here go hand in hand with the Philippians' joy. He wanted them to live a life of rejoicing, and he knew that nothing stifles thanksgiving like trying to live up to a standard you can never meet. So he warned them, "Look out!"

Yesterday we focused on the concept of circumcision to gain a better understanding of its cultural significance. Hopefully today you'll read this passage with greater insight as you consider Paul's warning to the Philippians.

Begin your time with prayer, asking God to help you understand the text.

Turn to page 125 and read **Philippians 3:1–11**.

1. Why do you think Paul commanded the Philippians to rejoice *in the Lord*? What else might they have rejoiced in?

2. How does offering thanksgiving help safeguard our souls? How does it fight against bitterness, envy, and discontentment?

When Paul used the terms *dogs* and *mutilators of the flesh* (NIV), he was referring to a certain group in early Christianity called Judaizers. This group believed that Gentiles (all those who were non-Jewish) needed to become Jewish in order to become Christians. Therefore, they required Gentile Christians to undergo circumcision.

As we discussed yesterday, circumcision was the outward sign of the covenant that God made with Abraham. His descendants were to receive circumcision on the eighth day (Leviticus 12:3) as a sign of being part of the covenant community and partakers in the blessings God promised to Abraham. While his descendants took on this outward sign, the true sign of a follower of God is (and always has been) a circumcised heart.

3. From what you read yesterday, why do you think Paul was so disturbed by the Judaizers? Where were they placing their confidence?

4. Why do you think he used the term *dogs*? Read the following for further insight:

For dogs encompass me;
  a company of evildoers encircles me;
they have pierced my hands and feet. (Psalm 22:16)

Outside are the dogs and sorcerers and the sexually immoral and murderers and idolaters, and everyone who loves and practices falsehood. (Revelation 22:15)

5. Why do you think Paul listed all the reasons he might have boasted in the flesh? How would this support his argument?

Paul had many reasons for boasting. Yet he considered them worthless. The term *rubbish* in this passage refers to the remains of a feast, thrown from the table. Usually it's the dogs that come and eat the leftovers. Paul used this imagery to illustrate how the Judaizers acted like dogs because they placed value in something worthless. Today it'd be like one of us considering ourselves rich because we have a stockpile of Monopoly money. We'd be putting our confidence in something that has no value!

6. Why do you think Paul was so upset by their teaching?

7. What was Paul's hope based on? Why?

8. Paul had great zeal as a Jewish leader. As a Christian, he continued to have zeal, but he aimed it in a new direction. What was he eager for now?

A friend recently hosted our family for dinner. When she invited us, I responded with "Oh, we'd love to come. What can we bring?" She insisted, "Nothing. I just want you to come and enjoy. I'll make everything." Truthfully, I felt uncomfortable receiving her gracious invitation. I wanted to bring something. It's difficult to simply come, with nothing to offer.

Similarly, we may be uncomfortable receiving the gospel, the good news of God's grace, freely given. We're invited, and we don't have anything to offer. As Isaiah 55:1–2 says,

> Come, everyone who thirsts,
>   come to the waters;
> and he who has no money,
>   come, buy and eat!
> Come, buy wine and milk
>   without money and without price.
> Why do you spend your money for that which is not bread,
>   and your labor for that which does not satisfy?
> Listen diligently to me, and eat what is good,
>   and delight yourselves in rich food.

We're invited to a delightful feast, but it's for the thirsty, those who are needy, the ones who have nothing to offer. That's you and me.

Yet just like the Judaizers, we try to bring something to the feast. They brought their outward circumcision and Jewish pedigree, hoping that they meant something. We attempt to bring things like our volunteer efforts, church attendance, monetary gifts, or baptism certificate. These outward signs are of no value without inward change and renewal. They aren't bad things (many of these are good things!), but they are ineffectual as the basis of our faith.

Paul understood that his own righteousness could never please God. He needed the righteousness of Christ. So do we.

Tomorrow we'll look at the ways we attempt to earn God's favor, the ways we try to live up to outward standards instead of humbly accepting the free gift that's offered. As the hymn "Rock of Ages" says so beautifully,

> Nothing in my hand I bring,
> Simply to Thy cross I cling.

Close your time today in prayer, rejoicing in the Lord, thanking Him for His free invitation of mercy and grace.

DAY 4: APPLICATION

How Does the Text Transform Me?

It's easy for us to look back at the Judaizers and find it strange that they put their confidence in something like circumcision. However, if you take a moment to consider our own culture, it's pretty clear we still put our confidence in our own abilities or attributes.

Some place their confidence in how carefully they eat or how many times they work out each week. Others place it in their intellect—what they read, what they know, where they studied. Some take confidence in their community service or involvement with the poor. Others find it in their families—how many children they have and how many activities they can get them to each day. And still others feel confident because of their finances, work, or social status.

We try in multiple ways to prove to others and to ourselves that we are virtuous or important. We also attempt to prove ourselves to God. We place confidence in our good works rather than in the righteousness only Christ can give.

This is a life-changing truth to understand: *God accepts you fully, completely, 100 percent on the merits of Christ.*

Your works (just like Paul's list of credentials) will never be enough to please God. Jesus gives us everything we need. And it's not just that our slate is wiped clean and we get to start over—it's that we're credited with all His good works. When we believe in Jesus, His righteousness is deposited into our account. It's way better than winning the lottery—we're given a perfect record. When God looks at you and me, He sees His dearly beloved Son in whom He is well pleased. It's for this very reason Paul wrote to the *saints* (not sinners) in Philippi.

This in no way means our good works don't matter. Remember in chapter 2 of his letter, Paul told the Philippians to work out their salvation with fear and trembling. Paul urged them to conduct themselves in a manner worthy of the gospel. Good works matter. However, good works are the *evidence* of God's work in us, not the *cause* of His love for us. If we misunderstand this important concept, we will lose our joy.

So today I want you to consider these questions in your own life: Where are you striving to please or impress others—or even God? In what areas are you trusting in your own merits? How do these efforts rob you of joy?

Begin your time in prayer, asking the Lord to show you how to apply this passage to your own life.

Read **Philippians 3:1–11** on page 125.

1. This passage begins with a command to rejoice *in the Lord*. Do you regularly give thanks to God *for God*? List three characteristics of the Lord for which you are thankful today.

2. How does a humble view of our own accomplishments lead us to greater joy in what Christ has done for us? By contrast, what are some results of a prideful view of our own accomplishments?

Essentially, Paul's warning against circumcision was rooted in a concern about placing more importance on a ritual than on a heart-level relationship with God. He was not opposed to circumcision, for he even encouraged Timothy to be circumcised before one of their missionary journeys (Acts 16). He was concerned about people placing their security in a ceremonial rite instead of in a relationship with Jesus.

3. What rituals do some people take confidence in today while neglecting a true relationship with God? How is this detrimental to one's faith as well as harmful to the church?

4. Take a moment to list several reasons that you could put "confidence in the flesh" like Paul. It could be your family name, where you grew up, your travels, your career, past awards, your ministry involvement, your income, your husband's job, your home, your university, or your children's accomplishments. List the areas in which you might be tempted to place your confidence.

5. Can you say you consider all those things rubbish in comparison to knowing Christ? Why or why not?

6. Paul's greatest desire and hope was to know Christ fully. Think through what your thoughts and energies are currently focused on. Is any of it distracting you from your relationship with Jesus? Explain the evidence either way. If something is taking priority over your relationship with Jesus, what solution might you consider?

7. Paul wanted to know Jesus even to the point of sharing in His sufferings and death. Can you think of a time when suffering caused your faith to grow? If so, how did it help you to know Christ in new ways?

In this passage, Paul contrasted a legalistic relationship with God and a grace-based relationship with God. A legalistic relationship is when a person tries to obtain God's favor by keeping the law. In hopes of being "good enough," the person does good works to please God and obtain favor. A grace-based relationship with God is the complete opposite. When a person believes in Christ, she is saved by faith. God welcomes her into His family based on Christ's life, not her own. She is fully accepted, and from that love she grows in greater love for God and for others.

8. In what ways are you trusting in your own good works to obtain God's favor? How does that lead to failure and frustration? How would a grace-based relationship with God increase your joy?

Paul listed a number of qualities that might have elevated his status. It's an impressive list, but he reckoned it all as worthless. He wasn't ashamed of these items, but he realized that they lacked value in God's economy. God looked with pleasure on Paul solely because of Christ. Paul was accepted into the family of God based on his faith alone. He didn't need to delight in the scraps thrown on the floor and given to the dogs. He could sit as a member of the family at the table, fully belonging to God. Therefore, he rejoiced in Christ and Christ alone.

9. Do you believe that you are fully acceptable to God because of Christ? If not, what holds you back from believing that God accepts you? If so, how is the true source of your confidence evident in your life?

10. If you believe that Christ died for you and fully accepts you, what keeps you from rejoicing?

God loves you. I know that's hard to believe sometimes. You might be tempted to say, "But, Melissa, you don't know what I've done. You can't imagine. I'm so ashamed."

You're right. I don't know what you've done. And you don't know all that I've done. But remember our author, Paul? He went after Christians, men and women, persecuting them with zeal, putting them in prison. He thought he was doing something right, but he was doing something terribly wrong. He may have had a pedigree, but he didn't have perfection. And Paul promised, "There is therefore now no condemnation for those who are in Christ Jesus. For the law of the Spirit of life has set you free in Christ Jesus from the law of sin and death" (Romans 8:1–2).

This is why Paul had so much joy: he knew he was free from condemnation! Jesus rescued him, saved him, and freed him. He wanted to know Jesus more and more because He's the way, the truth, and the life—the fullness that fills all things (John 14:6). The more we know Him, abide in Him, and spend time with Him, the more we experience abundant life. Apart from Jesus we can do nothing (15:5). With Jesus, we can do all things (Philippians 4:13).

Spend some time today asking the Lord to give you a heart that wants to know Christ above all else. Ask Him to expose the areas in which you're trusting in the rituals of the church or in your own merit instead of in a relationship with God.

Our joy is directly related to where we place our confidence and trust. Ask God to fill you with a new kind of joy.

DAY 5: DEVOTIONAL

Joy in Knowing Christ

Oh, taste and see that the LORD is good!

—PSALM 34:8

I love food. And every year that passes, I think I enjoy food a bit more. You might think that, after forty-some years of eating, I'd be bored. But I'm not. I keep finding new flavors and combinations of flavors that allow me to experience food in new ways. The more I cook, the more I understand the flavors I'm tasting—I relish the hints of rosemary, mint, cilantro, and sage. I love cooking for others because I delight in having friends sit at my table and share in the joy of tasting together.

The psalmist urges us, "Oh, taste and see that the LORD is good!" (Psalm 34:8). He wants us to savor the goodness of God like we savor a good meal. Just like our enjoyment of food, knowing Jesus doesn't get boring. In fact, the more we know Him, the more we want to know Him. When we taste His goodness, we want more and more of it. And we want to share Him with others.

One way to experience God's goodness is by being thankful. Rejoicing *in the Lord* is a safeguard for the soul. It protects us from finding our happiness in lesser things, as we set our minds on remembering and reflecting on what God has done. By focusing on God's work, we take our eyes off our own accomplishments. When we delight in God, we want to know Him more.

You can hear this hunger for a deeper relationship with Jesus in Paul's words. He wasn't satisfied with an outward display of religion. He wanted to know Jesus and keep knowing Him. He had found the source of living water, and he wanted to keep drinking.

Paul also understood the allure of those things that will never satisfy our thirst, so he warned, "Watch out for those dogs, those men who do evil, those mutilators of the flesh" (Philippians 3:2, NIV). Essentially, Paul was concerned about the threat of legalism—the attempt to be right before God by our own works. Legalists create an outward standard of behavior by which to judge themselves (and others). As they work to achieve their own standard, they consider themselves right before God. Like water poured over a roaring fire, legalism smothers joy in the hearts of believers. There's little joy when you feel as if you're working day in and day out to prove yourself. It's exhausting to never know if you're good enough.

As we learned this week, many legalists in Paul's day concerned themselves with circumcision, requiring it for all new believers. Called by the name Judaizers, these legalists taught that new converts needed to become Jewish before they could become Christians. Paul spoke so harshly against them because he knew they were placing confidence in their human efforts rather than in Christ—and requiring others to do the same.

In our day, legalism can take many different forms. We may be legalistic about worship, preaching, Sunday school attendance, personal devotions, school choices, where we live, how we parent, what we eat, or a myriad of other ways we seek to be better than others. We can even be legalistic about not being legalistic! Any time we place our pride and boasting in something other than Christ, we're likely to lose our joy.

In our fight against legalism, we may be tempted toward licentiousness. We question, "If our good works don't matter, then why should we obey God?" However, Paul never claimed that our works are of no value, nor did he lower the standard of our obedience. Our good works flow out of our union with Christ. We don't obey in order to earn our salvation. Nor do we disobey in order to show that we're free from the law. Rather, our salvation is by grace, and by grace we do good works that glorify God.

This focus on grace gives us a joy-filled thirst for more of Christ. The legalist thirsts in vain for self-righteousness, and the licentious person thirsts in vain for freedom. In Christ we find a righteousness apart from the law and a true freedom from the law's power. This discovery makes us thirsty for more.

You can hear this desire in Paul's cry, "I want to know Christ." Didn't Paul already know Christ? Yes, he knew Christ, but he realized his need for more of Him. Coming to Christ both fills our souls and makes us thirsty for more. Our joy grows as our knowledge and affection for Jesus grows.

Preacher and theologian A. W. Tozer spoke to this thirst in the following prayer. Use his words today to guide your prayers:

> O God, I have tasted Thy goodness, and it has both satisfied me and made me thirsty for more. I am painfully conscious of my need for further grace. I am ashamed of my lack of desire. O God, the Triune God, I want to want Thee; I long to be filled with longing; I thirst to be made more thirsty still."[1]

Amen.

Something Better Is Coming

Joy in Heaven

Philippians 3:12–4:1

Do I know my own real identity? My own real destiny? *I am a child of God. God is my Father; heaven is my home; every day is one day nearer. My Saviour is my brother; every Christian is my brother too.* Say it over and over to yourself first thing in the morning, last thing at night, as you wait for the bus, any time when your mind is free, and ask that you may be enabled to live as one who knows it is all utterly and completely true.

—J. I. Packer

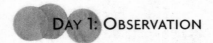

DAY 1: OBSERVATION

What Does the Text Say?

As I write today, it's a cold Saturday morning in February. To be honest, it was somewhat difficult to leave home and come to work. I wanted to sleep in and spend the morning sipping tea and enjoying a homemade breakfast with my family. However, I know this work is what the Lord has for me today, and that gives me a deep sense of purpose.

I'm also looking forward to something that gives me joy today as I work. This summer is our twentieth wedding anniversary, and my husband and I just booked a trip to the resort where we honeymooned. Our vacation is scheduled for the week after my manuscript is due. My work will be finished, and we can enjoy five days by ourselves looking out at the ocean. I'll sleep in, sip tea, read books, and enjoy long chats with my husband while listening to the waves crash on the shore. I cannot wait.

There's joy as we look forward to things. Children (and many of us adults too!) spend the month of December in hopeful anticipation of Christmas morning. As adults, we work diligently in our labors, looking forward to a paycheck at the end of the month. We clean, purge, and organize in hopes of a home that runs smoothly and stays tidy. We prepare a meal while anticipating the joy of savoring it with others.

Future hope gives present joy.

This week Paul's words will lead us to consider the hopeful anticipation of heaven. As we focus our minds on all that awaits us there, we'll increasingly experience joy here. There's nothing better to look forward to, nothing better coming our way, nothing more we could ever hope for than heaven.

Begin your time with prayer, asking for understanding and wisdom as you read the passage.

Read **Philippians 3:12–4:1**.

> [12]Not that I have already obtained this or am already perfect, but I
> press on to make it my own, because Christ Jesus has made me his own.

¹³Brothers, I do not consider that I have made it my own. But one thing I do: forgetting what lies behind and straining forward to what lies ahead, ¹⁴I press on toward the goal for the prize of the upward call of God in Christ Jesus. ¹⁵Let those of us who are mature think this way, and if in anything you think otherwise, God will reveal that also to you. ¹⁶Only let us hold true to what we have attained.

¹⁷Brothers, join in imitating me, and keep your eyes on those who walk according to the example you have in us. ¹⁸For many, of whom I have often told you and now tell you even with tears, walk as enemies of the cross of Christ. ¹⁹Their end is destruction, their god is their belly, and they glory in their shame, with minds set on earthly things. ²⁰But our citizenship is in heaven, and from it we await a Savior, the Lord Jesus Christ, ²¹who will transform our lowly body to be like his glorious body, by the power that enables him even to subject all things to himself.

⁴:¹Therefore, my brothers, whom I love and long for, my joy and crown, stand firm thus in the Lord, my beloved.

1. Think back (or look back) to the passage from last week. What had Paul not yet obtained?

2. What four things did he continue to do (verses 12–14)?

3. What did Paul ask his readers to do in verse 16?

4. Whose example did he ask them to follow?

5. How did Paul describe the present and future of those who live "as enemies of the cross of Christ"?

6. In contrast, where is the Christian's citizenship? How do Christians live?

7. How did Paul describe his feelings for the Philippians? What did he want them to do?

As I anticipate our twentieth-anniversary trip, I have no guarantee that everything will go smoothly. Flights might be delayed. Illness could strike. We might spend the week arguing. It could rain every day. Our carefully packed luggage might take a trip of its own to a different airport. I have expectations that may not be met.

By contrast, as I anticipate a future in heaven, my hope is set on something that's fully assured. Martyn Lloyd-Jones offered a glimpse of what we're looking forward to:

> We as Christian people are citizens of heaven. We belong to that realm
> and the day is coming when the King will return. Then we shall enter
> into our inheritance and we shall be completely changed. Sin will be
> entirely removed with all its effects and influences, and, perfect and
> glorified, we shall dwell with God in the glory for ever and ever. That
> is our birthright, that is our position.[1]

As followers of Jesus, we belong somewhere better than any place we can point to on a map. No country on earth can compare to the citizenship offered in heaven. Today, let your mind wander to your true home. As C. S. Lewis noted, "Joy is the serious business of Heaven."[2] Anticipate it. Look forward to it. Rest assured that a day is coming when all will be made right. Let it fill you with joy.

We may not experience the fullness of heaven today, but we can call home through prayer. Close your time today in prayer, knowing your words are heard by your Father in heaven (Revelation 8:3).

DAY 2: INTERPRETATION

What Does the Text Mean?

When my friend Angela first graduated from college, she worked as a bank teller. She spent weeks in training before actually working with customers. One thing that surprised me was the training method used to help employees spot counterfeit money. For weeks, the tellers only worked with real money. They were taught all that was true about each different bill—what special marks to look for on each one they received. They were never shown a counterfeit bill in the initial training.

Eventually, the trainers began to sneak in counterfeit bills alongside the real ones. Angela told me that after weeks of looking only at real bills, it was simple to spot the fakes, even the good ones. Her mind was so aware of what to look for, she could easily identify what was false, no matter how creative someone might be.

In a similar way, Paul wanted the Philippians to be aware of false teachers and know how to spot them. You and I need the same awareness today. Many men and women make a host of statements in the name of Christianity that are not biblical truths. We need to be able to discern the true gospel from counterfeit claims. As we immerse ourselves in truth, we'll be able to recognize the signs of real faith.

Open your time with prayer, asking the Lord to speak to you through the passage for today.

Turn back to pages 146–47 and read **Philippians 3:12–4:1**.

1. Why did Paul "press on," according to verse 12?

2. How did he go about pressing on in the faith?

3. Why do you think Paul chose to forget what lay behind him? What problems might have come from holding on to his past?

4. In this passage, Paul described himself as pressing on toward the goal to win the prize. What prize was Paul talking about?

5. What did Paul mean when he wrote, "Only let us hold true to what we have attained" (verse 16)?

6. Paul encouraged the Philippians to take his views and to follow his example. Does this mean Paul was not being humble? Explain your answer.

7. What did Paul mean when he said "their god is their belly" (verse 19) in describing those who live as enemies of Christ?

8. What did he mean by "they glory in their shame" (verse 19)?

9. Why would the belief that their citizenship is in heaven help and encourage the Philippians to stand firm in the Lord?

10. If the Philippians' citizenship was in heaven, how would that shape their view of their time on earth? (See 1 Peter 2:11.)

Paul's exhortations in this passage begin with right thinking (verse 15) and conclude with right living (verse 17). We live what we believe. As Martyn Lloyd-Jones said,

> Here is the Apostle's prescription for a happy, successful and full
> Christian life; be absolutely certain in your mind about the things
> that are vital, and the moment you are certain of them, put them into
> practice.[3]

If we live as citizens of heaven, we will value the priorities of our true home. But first we need to know what those priorities are, and Scripture is our guide. As you consider Paul's words, where do you need to grow in knowledge? Do you need to commit to learning the truths of Scripture in new ways? Do you need to read your Bible more, attend training opportunities, memorize Scripture, or commit to a Bible study so you can immerse yourself in the truth?

Or do you need to put into practice the truths you already know? Does your life match what you believe? In what ways are your concerns fixed on earthly things? How does that affect the choices you make? How would you like to live differently, more in line with what you believe?

Take these questions before the Lord today. Prayerfully ask Him to guide you in what you believe and how you live. Paul wrote to Timothy, "Keep a close watch on yourself and on the teaching" (1 Timothy 4:16). May we be women who faithfully do both.

DAY 3: INTERPRETATION

What Does the Text Mean?

Last week my husband looked up from his phone and told me the news I knew was coming but didn't want to hear. "Ruth just died." She'd been battling cancer for months, and we'd known that without a miracle her body would fail.

Even when we know something is coming, that doesn't protect us from the pain of the reality when it happens. Tears flowed around our breakfast table. My youngest shared, "I'm going to miss Mrs. Ruth opening up church." (Ruth often gave the congregational announcements on Sunday mornings.)

Mike and I headed to Ruth's home and joined others in praying together one last time around our friend. Her body was still there, but she was not. Her soul was with Jesus. I knew she was more alive at that moment than she'd ever been.

Knowing heaven awaits those who believe in Jesus brings comfort to the pain and loss we experience. In the midst of our sadness and tears, we feel a surprising sense of peace and joy for our loved one whose race is finished.

The reality of death also teaches us something about living. Ecclesiastes 7:2 explains, "It is better to go to the house of mourning than to go to the house of feasting, for this is the end of all mankind, and the living will lay it to heart."

As I held hands with friends around Ruth's bedside and prayed, her death and the thought of her arrival in heaven reminded me of what is important in life. The only thing that matters is knowing Jesus. I want to press on each day to know Jesus more and be like Him because heaven is my home and I look forward to spending eternity with Him. I want to tell others the good news because I know it's the most important news they'll ever hear. I want them to be in heaven with me.

As our gaze shifts from earthly concerns, we live differently, assured of our purpose. Today I want us to look at some other verses in Scripture that parallel Paul's desire for the Philippians to develop a heavenly perspective in order to stand firm and press on in the faith.

Read 1 Corinthians 15:42–58.

⁴²So is it with the resurrection of the dead. What is sown is perishable; what is raised is imperishable. ⁴³It is sown in dishonor; it is raised in glory. It is sown in weakness; it is raised in power. ⁴⁴It is sown a natural body; it is raised a spiritual body. If there is a natural body, there is also a spiritual body. ⁴⁵Thus it is written, "The first man Adam became a living being"; the last Adam became a life-giving spirit. ⁴⁶But it is not the spiritual that is first but the natural, and then the spiritual. ⁴⁷The first man was from the earth, a man of dust; the second man is from heaven. ⁴⁸As was the man of dust, so also are those who are of the dust, and as is the man of heaven, so also are those who are of heaven. ⁴⁹Just as we have borne the image of the man of dust, we shall also bear the image of the man of heaven.

⁵⁰I tell you this, brothers: flesh and blood cannot inherit the kingdom of God, nor does the perishable inherit the imperishable. ⁵¹Behold! I tell you a mystery. We shall not all sleep, but we shall all be changed, ⁵²in a moment, in the twinkling of an eye, at the last trumpet. For the trumpet will sound, and the dead will be raised imperishable, and we shall be changed. ⁵³For this perishable body must put on the imperishable, and this mortal body must put on immortality. ⁵⁴When the perishable puts on the imperishable, and the mortal puts on immortality, then shall come to pass the saying that is written:

"Death is swallowed up in victory."
⁵⁵"O death, where is your victory?
  O death, where is your sting?"

⁵⁶The sting of death is sin, and the power of sin is the law. ⁵⁷But thanks be to God, who gives us the victory through our Lord Jesus Christ.

⁵⁸Therefore, my beloved brothers, be steadfast, immovable, always abounding in the work of the Lord, knowing that in the Lord your labor is not in vain.

1. Paul discussed two types of bodies: natural and spiritual. List everything you learn from this passage about each.

   Natural Body   **Spiritual Body**

2. Paul also discussed the first Adam and the last Adam (Christ). List everything you learn about each of them.

   First Adam   **Last Adam (Christ)**

3. Describe the mystery Paul spoke of in this passage.

4. After Paul wrote about the glory of our new heavenly bodies, he gave the Corinthians a command similar to the one he gave in Philippians 4:1. What command did he give in 1 Corinthians 15:58? What assurance did he give about the outcome of their obedience?

Heavenly minded living doesn't mean apathetic living. We don't rest on our laurels waiting for Jesus to come back. We take all we've been given here—our time, talents, and resources—and we put them to use as we press on in the faith. We live with mission and purpose. Rather than allow earthly matters to consume our minds, we focus on what's eternally significant. We seek to live out God's kingdom, not build our own. We share our faith because we know it's the most important possession we have to offer others.

Heavenly minded living also gives us perspective on our lives and the trials we face. Read 2 Corinthians 4:6–10, 16–18.

> [6]For God, who said, "Let light shine out of darkness," has shone in our hearts to give the light of the knowledge of the glory of God in the face of Jesus Christ.
>
> [7]But we have this treasure in jars of clay, to show that the surpassing power belongs to God and not to us. [8]We are afflicted in every way, but not crushed; perplexed, but not driven to despair; [9]persecuted, but not forsaken; struck down, but not destroyed; [10]always carrying in the body the death of Jesus, so that the life of Jesus may also be manifested in our bodies. . . .
>
> [16]So we do not lose heart. Though our outer self is wasting away, our inner self is being renewed day by day. [17]For this light momentary affliction is preparing for us an eternal weight of glory beyond all comparison, [18]as we look not to the things that are seen but to the things that are unseen. For the things that are seen are transient, but the things that are unseen are eternal.

5. What do you think Paul meant by the statement "we have this treasure in jars of clay"? What is the treasure? What are the jars?

6. According to verses 8–10, what challenges did Paul face?

7. In the midst of these circumstances, why did Paul not lose heart?

8. What did he fix his eyes on, and why?

It's easy to become discouraged. Circumstances overwhelm. Future uncertainty sparks fear. Relationships disappoint. Unrealized expectations threaten our joy. If this world is all there is, we'd be right to despair. Thankfully, we have another home, a better one. All we face today is part of the journey. And as we all know, traveling is often uncomfortable. Things don't always go as planned. Patience wears thin. At times, we're separated from loved ones. Delays cause frustration. The journey may grow wearisome.

However, Paul reminded us we have something better to look forward to. These earthly aches and pains are temporary. We can journey with joy because home—with all its comforts and pleasures—is coming. These bodies may wear out, but we'll be given new ones.

Revelation pulls back the veil and gives us a glimpse of what awaits.

> Then I saw a new heaven and a new earth, for the first heaven and the
> first earth had passed away, and the sea was no more. ²And I saw the
> holy city, new Jerusalem, coming down out of heaven from God,
> prepared as a bride adorned for her husband. ³And I heard a loud
> voice from the throne saying, "Behold, the dwelling place of God is
> with man. He will dwell with them, and they will be his people, and
> God himself will be with them as their God. ⁴He will wipe away every
> tear from their eyes, and death shall be no more, neither shall there be
> mourning, nor crying, nor pain anymore, for the former things have
> passed away." (21:1–4)

This morning, close your time by thanking Jesus for securing and preparing such a place for each of us. No matter what happens on the journey, we're on our way home.

DAY 4: APPLICATION

How Does the Text Transform Me?

Last week we read Paul's warning against the threat of legalism, and we learned that it's impossible to secure God's favor by outward actions and keeping the law. We need the righteousness of Christ, and Christ alone, to be right with God. If we attempt to live up to a standard we can never keep, our lives will be joyless and hopeless.

In this week's reading, Paul alerted the Philippians to another danger: thinking that growth in the Christian life is passive. Paul didn't want them to wrongly conclude that because they'd been given the righteousness of Christ, there was no room for spiritual growth. Paul readily admitted his own shortcomings, but he determined to daily press on toward the goal. He wasn't sitting around waiting for God to instantaneously change him. He strained forward to what waited ahead. He was fully assured *and* fully motivated. He was zealous, diligent. He actively pursued being like Christ because God had promised to make him Christlike. And he wanted the Philippians (and us) to follow his example. He knew that taking hold of Christ meant taking hold of joy. Pressing on toward this goal is the best way to live.

As Martyn Lloyd-Jones noted,

> The Apostle says, "One thing I do"; it is regular and it is constant. The Christian life is impossible without discipline. We must control ourselves, we must divide up our time, we must realise, in a world that is so set against us, that if we do not discipline our spiritual life we shall certainly find ourselves in trouble.[4]

So let's read this week's text from Philippians again, seeking to apply it to our own lives. Ask the Lord for wisdom to understand the ways this passage can transform your life today.

Turn back to pages 146–47 and read **Philippians 3:12–4:1**.

1. Paul freely admitted he wasn't perfect. He still struggled with the reality of sin in his own life. Yet he pressed on, knowing Jesus had made him His own.

   a. Where do you struggle with sin in your life? It could be anger, impatience, gossip, unkindness, judgmental thoughts, lust, greed, envy. Where do you long to live with greater freedom from sin?

   b. How have you seen sin rob you of joy?

   c. How can you press on to fight the sin patterns you see? What are some practical changes that could help you?

2. Paul told the Philippians that he pressed on by "forgetting what lies behind and straining forward to what lies ahead" (verse 13).

   a. What do you need to forget from your past in order to grow in your faith today?

b. Paul used the term *straining* to describe his pursuit of God. He indicated active exertion, but he wasn't trying to earn God's favor. Instead, because he already had God's favor, he worked diligently to take hold of what had been promised. Are you actively pursuing God? In what ways? How can you more actively exert yourself to know Him?

3. Paul called the Philippians to follow his example and to take note of those who lived according to the pattern he and Timothy gave them. He wasn't calling the Philippians to imitate his faults but to follow his pattern of faith.

a. Why do we have to be careful to imitate others only insofar as they imitate and live like Christ?

b. What is our standard to know how Christ would want us to live?

c. Who do you know who understands the Bible well and lives his or her life according to its teachings?

d. What can you observe from this individual's life that you admire?

    e. Why is it important to have godly examples in our lives?

4. Paul warned against teachers with wrong motives. Have you ever been influenced by false teaching? How did that affect your faith?

5. What helped you to recognize and turn away from false teaching?

6. How do earthly cares distract you and keep you from rejoicing in the Lord? How do they fill you with worry and anxiety?

7. How does believing that your citizenship is in heaven shape how you live here on earth?

8. In what ways would setting your mind on heavenly things today change your outlook on life? What would bother you less? What would you seek to do more?

Paul reminded the Philippians to not waver in following God. It's difficult to do, isn't it? We're tempted toward self-focus and easy choices. Often I want to go my own way and fulfill my own desires. I want to focus on myself. Some so-called Christian teachers wrongly encourage this by teaching a health-and-wealth gospel focused on earthly gains. Paul warned us to be on our guard against them.

Knowing that self-focus never leads to lasting joy, Paul urged us to shift our gaze to something better, something secure. We need a vision of what's coming so that we'll treasure what's eternal. Right longings lead to righteous living. As the Puritan theologian John Owen encouraged, "Look to the vigor of the affections toward heavenly things; if they are not constantly attended, excited, directed and warned, they are apt to decay, and sin lies in wait to take every advantage against them."[5]

We don't naturally drift toward holiness. We have to deliberately press on toward it, knowing that God promises to work in and through us. Because He's in the process of making us like Jesus, we can strive with all that is in us to be more like Him.

Close in prayer today, asking God to renew in your heart an affection for heavenly things. Direct your gaze upward and shift your focus from the cares of this world to the promises of heaven. Praise God for the citizenship you've been granted.

Day 5: Devotional

Joy in the Journey

You make known to me the path of life;
    in your presence there is fullness of joy;
    at your right hand are pleasures forevermore.

—Psalm 16:11

A few years ago, my family and I lived overseas for a semester in Cambridge, England. Our home was full of old-world charm but short on modern American conveniences. The kitchen lacked a dishwasher and featured a dorm-sized refrigerator.

(It was like playing Tetris each time I returned from the store.) Our living space was smaller; we shared one bathroom among the six people living under one roof. Added to this was the need to cook from scratch every day because certain ingredients and cooking helps were unavailable. I even made my own Italian sausage at one point so I could make lasagna.

We walked most places because parking was scarce and driving was fairly stressful. On my first driving expedition, I was thankful to have broken only one major traffic law. Each time I opened my mouth to speak, others knew I was from somewhere else. Life was different and in many ways more difficult.

However, the daily struggles felt light and momentary. I remember standing at the sink (for hours), listening with delight to my children's voices as they played in the garden outside the kitchen window. The addition of daily tasks, the experience of being a foreigner, and the other inconveniences failed to consume my joy because of one simple thing: perspective.

I knew that my time in Cambridge was short. I realized we would be there only a little while, and I wanted to focus on the uniqueness of the experience instead of the difficulties. I also knew I had a wonderful home, dear friends, and a car that drove on the right side of the road awaiting me back in Charlotte. Knowing what was ours in Charlotte brought comfort in Cambridge, even though we were far from home.

In a similar desire for perspective, Paul encouraged the Philippians to turn their minds from earthly things and consider their heavenly citizenship. He knew their current situation was difficult, fraught with trials. So he reminded them that they were not yet home; they were strangers in a foreign land. They were supposed to live differently and speak differently than those around them, and so it was natural for them to feel out of place.

Paul pointed them to a life of hopeful waiting: waiting for Jesus to return and take them to their true home, where there would be no death, no tears, and no pain. Knowing what is ours in heaven brings comfort on earth, even when our true home seems far away. By contrast, the more we strive to make this world our home, the more difficult it is to live with joy.

Consider this challenge from the Puritan hymn-writer and theologian Richard Baxter:

O that Christians would learn to live with one eye on Christ crucified and the other on his coming in glory! If everlasting joys were more in your thoughts, spiritual joys would abound more in your hearts. No wonder you are comfortless when heaven is forgotten. When Christians let fall their heavenly expectations but heighten their earthly desires, they are preparing themselves for fear and trouble. Who has met with a distressed, complaining soul, where either a low expectation of heavenly blessings, or too high a hope for joy on earth is not present? What keeps us under trouble is either we do not expect what God has promised, or we expect what he did not promise.[6]

There's so much in our world to enjoy: sunsets at the beach, ice cream on a hot day, s'mores by a warm fire, the hug of a loved one, a friend's laughter—the world God made is filled with beauty and goodness. It's tempting to think that if we could just acquire *more,* we'd find what we're looking for here. While we can savor these gifts, they can't satisfy us. God is the source of all that's good, and all the good things He made point us back to Him.

God's Word keeps us focused on what's important. Our lives are not about gaining but giving, not about selfish pursuits but selfless service. We lay aside the past—both our failures and achievements—and strain forward toward the hope of heaven. We labor here, knowing that our rest is coming. Remembering and reflecting on the coming resurrection brings joy in the midst of a world where waiting, longing, pain, and suffering are common struggles in each of our lives.

The apostle John caught a glimpse of what was coming. In the book of Revelation, he described how one day God will dwell with people. And on that day, God will wipe away our tears. Death, mourning, crying, and pain will be no more. He's going to make everything new. It's difficult to even imagine a world like that, isn't it?

John also saw the river of the water of life flowing from the throne of God:

> On each side of the river stood the tree of life, bearing twelve crops of fruit, yielding its fruit every month. And the leaves of the tree are for the healing of the nations. *No longer will there be any curse.* The throne of

God and of the Lamb will be in the city, and his servants will serve him.
They will see his face, and his name will be on their foreheads. There
will be no more night. They will not need the light of a lamp or the light
of the sun, for the Lord God will give them light. And they will reign
forever and ever. (Revelation 22:2–5, NIV)

There will be no more sin, no more tears. The curse we have suffered under
since Eden will be no more. The nations will be healed. We will see the face of God.
What a hopeful vision. What a day that will be. Come, Lord Jesus.

C. S. Lewis wisely noted, "Aim at Heaven and you will get earth 'thrown in':
aim at earth and you will get neither."[7] Close your time in prayer today and consider
the following two questions:

1. How can I live my life aiming for heaven?

2. How can I press on to be more like Christ?

Whatever you face today, rejoice. We're almost home.

Week 8

A Heart at Peace

Joy in the Inner Life

Philippians 4:2–9

Through our petitions, we receive peace and rest. Just as physical sleep is "giving up control," so petition is giving up control, a resting and trusting in God to care for our needs. We must pray not only with shameless assertiveness but, at the same time, with a restful submissiveness, a confidence that God is wiser than we are and wants the best for us.

—Timothy Keller

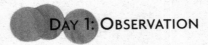

DAY 1: OBSERVATION

What Does the Text Say?

Facebook isn't what it used to be. When I originally joined, I loved catching up with old friends, seeing pictures of their families, and gaining glimpses into their lives. It felt like opening a scrapbook and getting to see how other people's stories had progressed after they moved on from my own.

Currently, my Facebook feed feels less like a scrapbook and more like a war zone. There's relational discord, political anxiety, and harsh commentary on just about everyone and everything in the public sphere. Overall, what I see is a lack of peace: relationally, emotionally, and spiritually. It's unsettling to witness so much anger, frustration, and anxiety.

What's shared publicly often reflects what's happening in our own lives. We feel conflicted, unsettled, and worried. We all have relational struggles and inward concerns that eat away at our joy. This week, we'll be looking at the ways the Lord offers peace in our relationships, our prayers, and our thinking. When peace reigns inwardly, we find it easier to rejoice outwardly.

Open your time with prayer, asking the Lord to give you wisdom and insight as you read the passage today.

Read **Philippians 4:2–9.**

> [2]I entreat Euodia and I entreat Syntyche to agree in the Lord. [3]Yes, I ask you also, true companion, help these women, who have labored side by side with me in the gospel together with Clement and the rest of my fellow workers, whose names are in the book of life.
>
> [4]Rejoice in the Lord always; again I will say, rejoice. [5]Let your reasonableness be known to everyone. The Lord is at hand; [6]do not be anxious about anything, but in everything by prayer and supplication with thanksgiving let your requests be made known to God. [7]And the peace of God, which surpasses all understanding, will guard your hearts and your minds in Christ Jesus.

⁸Finally, brothers, whatever is true, whatever is honorable, whatever is just, whatever is pure, whatever is lovely, whatever is commendable, if there is any excellence, if there is anything worthy of praise, think about these things. ⁹What you have learned and received and heard and seen in me—practice these things, and the God of peace will be with you.

1. What did Paul ask of Euodia and Syntyche?

2. Paul also wrote directly to his "true companion." While it's uncertain precisely who this person was, some commentators believe it was Luke, who originally traveled with Paul to Philippi and could have been staying there, according to the timeline of his travels and writings. What did Paul ask of his true companion?

3. What additional information did Paul give about Euodia and Syntyche?

4. In verses 4–9 Paul gave six commands. List them below.

5. What do you learn from this passage about the Lord and how He interacts with us?

6. What type of things did Paul want his readers to think about?

7. What did Paul want the Philippians to put into practice? In other words, how did he want them to live?

The mind is powerful. Our thoughts can rehearse past hurts, recite present anxieties, and ruminate over potential future troubles in our world. Round and round we spiral, sinking downward into discouragement or even despair. The fruit of such thinking is frustration, anger, hopelessness, and worry. This is not the way of peace.

Thankfully, when we submit our thoughts to Him, God transforms the way we think about the world and then uses us to transform the world. In the Lord, we can experience relational unity, emotional peace, and a new way of thinking.

Paul understood the power of the mind as he wrote to the Corinthians, "We destroy arguments and every lofty opinion raised against the knowledge of God, and take every thought captive to obey Christ" (2 Corinthians 10:5). Paul employed military language to describe the battle going on in his mind. He was at war—chasing down his thoughts and taking them captive. He didn't simply follow his own opinions or impressions; he examined them through the lens of what is true and right.

We need to do the same. How we think about others, our circumstances, and the world around us—it matters. And our vision isn't always clear. We need the lens of Scripture to help us view the world with clarity and truth. When a false thought pops into our minds, we need to take it captive.

Today you may think there's nothing lovely or praiseworthy in your life. You may think it's impossible to rejoice. These are thoughts to take captive and view through the lens of the Bible. Paul's exhortation to rejoice isn't centered on the circumstances of your life; it's centered on the greatness of your God. That's why Paul commanded us (once again) to rejoice *in the Lord.*

God created you, sought you, redeemed you, and one day He will bring you home. These truths are the foundation of a life of peace and joy. With God as the focus, there are always reasons to rejoice.

Consider this challenge from Martyn Lloyd-Jones:

My friend, if your name is written in heaven, if you belong to him, your reward is absolutely certain. There is joy in glory awaiting you that you cannot imagine or conceive. So, then, remember that he is coming, the Lord is at hand—keep looking at that. . . .

Above all, contemplate being with him, spending eternity in his glorious presence, and sharing in that joy that is set before him.[1]

Spend some time today praising God. Meditate on His goodness, His greatness, His glory. If you are struggling with a lack of peace or lack of joy today, tell Him. Ask Him to refresh and revive your heart.

Day 2: Interpretation

What Does the Text Mean?

I'm thankful for the rich gospel partnerships I've shared with other women. These friendships have blessed my life in tremendous ways. Yet there's also the reality that some relationships with other believers are difficult. I've been hurt by unkind words, gossip, and uncharitable assumptions. I'm sure I've hurt others in similar ways.

These relational strains can turn into schisms that damage the church. Pursuing healthy friendships with one another is important, even when it's hard. Often I've found the Lord uses difficult relationships to show me my own sin and the areas where He's working on my heart. I think *she* needs to change, and the Lord shows me *I'm* the one who needs to change!

Living in community isn't easy. Believers can hold grudges, speak unkindly, and just plain not like one another for a variety of reasons. Perhaps someone immediately comes to mind as you read these words. Whom do you struggle to get along with? Is there someone with whom you regularly have personality conflicts?

Begin your time praying for that person. Ask the Lord to give you insight, understanding, and a soft heart. Pray that He would lead and guide you through this passage today, giving you discernment as you read.

Turn back to pages 166–67 and read **Philippians 4:2–9.**

1. Why do you think Paul was concerned for Euodia and Syntyche to agree with each other in the Lord?

2. What's the difference between agreeing with one another for the sake of unity in Christ and just pretending to get along in order to ignore an underlying problem?

3. How might disunity among leaders in the church affect the church body?

4. What does this passage teach you about Paul's perspective on women participating and being leaders in the church?

5. Why do you think Paul commanded them once again to rejoice? Why do we at times need to be commanded to rejoice?

6. What is the difference between rejoicing in the Lord and rejoicing in our circumstances?

7. What does it mean to "let your reasonableness be known to everyone"? Why is that important as we live and work with others?

8. How does the Lord's nearness encourage us toward rejoicing and away from anxiety?

9. What command did Paul give in connection with anxiety?

10. What does anxiety reveal about our relationship with God?

11. What do the following verses reveal about the difference between godly concern and fretful anxiety?

"Father, if you are willing, remove this cup from me. Nevertheless, not my will, but yours, be done." And there appeared to him an angel from heaven, strengthening him. And being in agony he prayed more earnestly; and his sweat became like great drops of blood falling down to the ground. (Luke 22:42–44)

I have thought it necessary to send to you Epaphroditus my brother and fellow worker and fellow soldier, and your messenger and minister to my need, for he has been longing for you all and has been distressed because you heard that he was ill. Indeed he was ill, near to death. But God had mercy on him, and not only on him but on me also, lest I should have sorrow upon sorrow. I am the more eager to send him, therefore, that

you may rejoice at seeing him again, and that I may be less anxious.
(Philippians 2:25–28)

   a. How is this kind of anxiety different from the anxiety Paul cautioned
       against?

   b. What do you learn from these two examples that you can apply to
       your own life?

12. What does prayer involve, according to Philippians 4:6?

13. Why is prayer helpful when we are anxious or worried?

14. How does peace guard our hearts? In what ways have you found this to
    be true?

A good friend was recently diagnosed with stage 4 breast cancer. I want to
somehow make her better, but I can't. My mind quickly races down the "what if"
rabbit trail of worry. I have to fight my brain's active imagination and turn my fears
and concerns to the Lord in prayer. And somehow, through prayer, God guards my
heart.

The Greek word for "guard" in this passage describes the duty of a warrior. It's a military term. As the nineteenth-century English theologian J. B. Lightfoot explained, "God's peace shall stand sentry, shall keep guard over your hearts."[2]

Our world is full of concerns (both real and imagined) that want to steal our peace. And just like both Jesus and Paul, we face troubling circumstances; hardships, struggles, and anxieties are part of life in this world. How do we handle the fears we face? In the agonizing moments before Jesus went to the cross, He set an example for us: He prayed.

That's exactly what Paul instructed us to do with our worry and anxieties. Rather than ruminate over and over about them in our minds (which often amplifies our anxiety), we pray and give our concerns over to God. He has the power to give us peace in the most unsettling circumstances.

Pause now and bring your anxieties to the Lord. Take your requests to Him in prayer, asking for His peace to guard your heart and mind. Also, spend time in thanksgiving, thinking through all He has done for you. Rejoice in Him today, even as you lay your cares before Him.

DAY 3: INTERPRETATION

What Does the Text Mean?

My daughter had a rough day at school last week. She came home and told me all about it. As she recounted friendship struggles and academic frustrations, her face reflected her dismay. I listened and sympathized, but when she finished relating her challenges, she seemed more disheartened than when she'd begun.

I continued our discussion with a simple question, "Can you tell me a few things that you're happy about today? Let's try to find ten things that were good in your day." I wasn't attempting to gloss over what was hard, but I wanted to help her see that alongside the difficulties there were blessings.

As we chatted, she listed some of the good things that had happened, and with each one her face seemed a little less droopy. By the end, we were laughing together, and she said, "I guess there were a lot of good things in my day too."

What we think about matters, doesn't it? We can focus on what's disappointing, frustrating, and painful, or we can think about what's good, right, and praiseworthy. A choice lies before you today: where will you set the dial of your mind? Begin right now. What are you thinking about? Are you anxious or worried about something? Are you facing a decision and you don't know what to do? In the midst of all you can't control, take your concerns to God. He listens and He's able. He can provide just what you need, even when it seems impossible.

How we think determines how we live. So today we are going to focus in on Philippians 4:8–9. To better understand Paul's direction to believers, we're going to examine these verses closely, looking at each specific word. You'll need a dictionary, either digital or print. Before you begin, open your time with prayer, asking the Spirit to guide you as you meditate on God's Word.

Read **Philippians 4:8.**

> Finally, brothers, whatever is true, whatever is honorable, whatever is just, whatever is pure, whatever is lovely, whatever is commendable, if there is any excellence, if there is anything worthy of praise, think about these things.

1. Look up each of the following words in a dictionary and write a short definition:

   a. True:

   b. Honorable:

   c. Just:

d. Pure:

e. Lovely:

f. Commendable:

g. Excellent:

h. Praiseworthy:

2. What did you learn as you looked up the definitions of these words? What, if anything, surprised you or interested you in particular?

3. How does considering what is true, honorable, and just help when we're feeling anxious about something?

4. How does filling our minds with excellent and praiseworthy thoughts help us to overflow with joy and thanksgiving?

5. Why did Paul want his readers to put into practice what they had learned? What is the danger of learning a lot about God without putting it into practice in our own lives?

6. Spend the rest of your time today in prayer. Go through each of these words again, and write down one characteristic of God, His church, or His actions toward you that reflects each of these categories. Then praise God for each item.

   a. True:

   b. Honorable:

   c. Just:

   d. Pure:

   e. Lovely:

f. Commendable:

g. Excellent:

h. Praiseworthy:

As you go through your day, think on these things. May the Lord fill your mind with peace and joy. End your time today with the following prayer:

> Let the words of my mouth and the meditation of my heart
>> be acceptable in your sight,
> O Lord, my rock and my redeemer. (Psalm 19:14)

Day 4: Application

How Does the Text Transform Me?

One of my favorite passages in Scripture is Habakkuk 3:16–19. The prophet Habakkuk knew an invading army was heading for Israel to carry out God's punishment for the disobedient nation. He knew suffering was coming. He had good reason to be anxious and fearful. This is what he wrote:

> Yet I will quietly wait for the day of trouble
>> to come upon people who invade us.
> Though the fig tree should not blossom,
>> nor fruit be on the vines,
> the produce of the olive fail

and the fields yield no food,
the flock be cut off from the fold
    and there be no herd in the stalls,
yet I will rejoice in the LORD;
    I will take joy in the God of my salvation.
GOD, the Lord, is my strength;
    he makes my feet like the deer's;
    he makes me tread on my high places.

Habakkuk acknowledged what was coming: a lack of fruit on the vines, barren fields, and decimated flocks. Complete devastation. He didn't try to gloss over the painful realities to make his situation appear less difficult.

However, in the midst of it all, he rejoiced in the Lord. His joy wasn't rooted in his circumstances but in his salvation: "I will take joy in the God of my salvation." No one could steal his joy because the object of his rejoicing (God's salvation) was secure.

I want to learn Habakkuk's secret of contentment so fully that when life is overwhelmingly hard, God's strength overflows in abiding joy. As God's peace reigns in our hearts, His praise will be on our lips. No matter what happens, we can always rejoice *in the Lord* because He is always full of goodness, love, mercy, kindness, and grace.

He is worthy. May we be willing.

Today we'll look at how to apply these truths in our own lives. Open your time in prayer, asking the Lord to guide, convict, and encourage you as you study today.

Turn once more to pages 166–67, or open your Bible, and read **Philippians 4:2–9.**

1. Have you been affected by disagreements among leadership in the church? How have you seen disunity harm the body of Christ? (I encourage you to keep your answer to this question and the next one private.)

2. Do you currently feel disunity with any believer? Or do you know of people who are at odds with one another? How can you work to build unity in your own relationships and in other people's relationships?

3. What would it look like in your life to "rejoice in the Lord" more in your thoughts? Your words? Your actions?

Paul counseled believers to nurture an attitude toward God that was full of rejoicing and an attitude toward one another that was full of reasonableness (or "gentleness," as the NIV translates it). This doesn't mean we sweep relational problems under the rug, ignore sin patterns, or dismiss important doctrinal issues. In the preceding passage, Paul warned the Philippians to be on their guard against false teachers. However, there's a difference between disagreements in the church about matters of primary importance (like the gospel) and disputable matters (like worship styles).

As we seek wisdom in matters that aren't clearly discussed in Scripture, or as we deal with the mistakes of others, we can do so with kindness, patience, and humility. Scholar L. H. Marshall described reasonableness as "fairmindedness, the attitude of a man who is charitable towards men's faults and merciful in his judgment of their failings because he takes their whole situation into his reckoning."[3]

4. Would you describe yourself as charitable toward others' faults? Is there anyone with whom you struggle to have a spirit of gentleness? Why do you think that is?

5. Who is an example to you of the type of reasonableness Paul encouraged? What about that person do you admire?

6. When you are anxious and worried, how do you typically cope? Do you call your best friend or husband and talk it out? Do you take charge and get to work solving the problem on your own? Do you go shopping to distract yourself? Do you withdraw and quietly fret? Do you act out in anger toward others? Or maybe you eat an entire bag of chips or a container of ice cream?

7. What would it look like for you to take your concerns to the Lord in prayer? How can you incorporate prayer into your daily routine?

The term *prayer* in the Greek is *proseuchē,* while the term *petition* is *deēsis.* The following quote offers a helpful explanation of the differences between the two words: "*Proseuchē* is used of prayer in general, while *deēsis* gives prominence to the sense of need. On the other hand, *deēsis* is used as well of requests from man to man, while *proseuchē* is limited to prayer to God."[4] From this explanation, we understand that petitions are a specific type of prayer, a coming to God with our needs.

8. What specific needs are you facing today that you can bring before the Lord?

9. If you can, think of a time you experienced the peace of God in the midst of difficult circumstances. What role did your prayers or the prayers of others play in bringing about that peace?

10. Take a moment to think through what you feed your mind each day—the television shows you watch, the magazines you read, the websites you surf. Are they helping you to think about things that are excellent or praiseworthy? What changes can you make to help you focus your mind on that which is true, lovely, honorable, and just?

11. Often I know what I'm supposed to do (be prayerful, think rightly, read my Bible, be patient, rejoice in the Lord), but I struggle to actually do it. What could you do today to put into practice what you know to be true?

It's easy to read this passage and think to ourselves, *Well, that's so simple! I'm going to take my concerns to the Lord in prayer, and I'm going turn my mind toward good, right, and lovely things.* However, if you're like me, what's simple to understand is often difficult to actually *live out.*

Think about how simple it is to lose weight—you just eat properly and exercise, right? It's simple to understand but so very difficult to do!

What's true about our physical lives is often reflected in our spiritual lives—what sounds simple is often difficult to do. We naturally try to run our own lives. We feel like all the responsibility for every single thing is on us. It's difficult to put down our phones, stop solving all the world's problems, and still our hearts before God. It's much easier to rehash everything that went wrong in our day, to stress about the state of the world, and to fret about those we love.

To help me quiet my heart before God, I've found it helpful to write out my prayers. As I take my pen in hand, my thoughts slow down. I pour out my concerns, my anxieties, and my distress. Slowly I remember I'm not the one in control—God is. There are so many things I have no power over. There's so much I can't change. But God can.

As I meditate on who God is and what He can do, my mind is filled with that which is lovely, right, and true. Even when my heart is weighed down with hardship, thinking about God causes me to rejoice. I can't help but give thanks when I consider who He is and what He's done for me. He's rescued me. He's saved me. He's promised to come back for me and take me home. Thanksgiving walks side by side with the petitions I have for God.

Stillness and quiet allow God's Word to direct our prayers and guide our thoughts. Take ten minutes right now to pray. If you've never written out your prayers, why not give it a try? Write to God as you'd write a letter to a friend. Tell Him all your cares and anxieties.

Take hold of these two promises: the peace of God will guard your heart, and the God of peace is with you. In Jesus, and in Jesus alone, is the peace we crave: "I have said these things to you, that in me you may have peace. In the world you will have tribulation. But take heart; I have overcome the world" (John 16:33).

May His peace be yours today.

Day 5: Devotional

Joy in the Inner Life

> Peace I leave with you; my peace I give to you. Not as the world gives do I give to you. Let not your hearts be troubled, neither let them be afraid.
>
> —John 14:27

Peace. It's something we all want, isn't it? And I can easily envision what it might look like:

- an hour to myself, sitting on a hammock, the sun on my face, and a gentle breeze blowing while I read a book
- a home where all the beds are made, the dishes are put away, and all the closets are organized neatly
- a family dinner with everyone laughing, enjoying one another, and using kind words

Many of the ways I search for peace involve arranging my circumstances and people so there's nothing to complicate, bother, or disturb. However, life doesn't usually cooperate with my plans. The hammock is probably a breeding ground for mosquitoes, the neatly made beds last for one day, and family dinners all too easily turn into selfish discussions of who gets the last piece of pie. Outer circumstances can't produce lasting inward peace.

Paul described a different sort of peace than what we often imagine. He encouraged the Philippians (and us) toward peaceful living—in both outward relationships and inward thoughts. First of all, he wanted Euodia and Syntyche "to agree *in the Lord.*" He was not asking them to sacrifice truth or doctrine in order to come to an agreement. He didn't advise them to agree for agreement's sake. Rather, Paul encouraged them to get along as they worked together for the cause of the gospel—to be at peace with each other.

Most likely petty disputes between these two women were causing unnecessary divisions in the church. Paul acknowledged that both women were partakers of the grace of Christ and fellow laborers for His kingdom. It's a helpful reminder that sometimes our leaders will be at odds with one another over disputable matters. Rather than join one side or the other, we can help bring peaceful resolution and agreement in the Lord. As Proverbs 15:18 tells us, "A hot-tempered man stirs up dissension, but a patient man calms a quarrel" (NIV). Our words and actions can stifle dissension and encourage peace.

Second, Paul called the Philippians to an inner peace free from anxiety and worry. Paul wasn't insisting the Philippians put on a Pollyanna smile or a stiff upper lip in order to deal with the stresses of life. He recognized that they faced true struggles and concerns, just as he did. However, Paul knew that anxious fretting doesn't amount to much other than making us (and those around us) miserable. So he directed us toward a better way of dealing with our inner unrest: prayer and petition, along with thanksgiving. And he promised that God's peace will guard our hearts in a way that is beyond understanding.

Have you ever experienced that type of unexplainable peace? A few years ago, my father had a heart attack, which led to major bleeding in his brain. My brother and I drove for four hours in heavy traffic, wondering all the way if our dad would survive until we got to the hospital. As we drove, the phone conversations we had with friends of my mom prepared us for the worst. We had no power to do anything except pray and ask others to pray for my dad.

In the hours, days, and weeks that followed, an inner calm enveloped me that I couldn't understand or explain. God's peace set a guard over my heart in the midst of the unknown. We had very few answers in those days and many tears, but peace remained. I knew so many people were praying for our family, and at each step in the journey we felt the presence of the Lord. By God's grace, my dad survived. However, I felt the miracle of God's peace long before I experienced the miracle of my dad's survival.

Prayer is God's means for giving us unshakeable inner joy even when we're surrounded by external struggles and hardships. The peace of Jesus is different than anything the world can offer.

In addition to prayer, Paul exhorted the Philippians toward right thinking as another means for escaping their anxiety. Essentially, the first three words emphasized in 4:8—*true, honorable,* and *just*—speak to right doctrine. In Scripture we find life-giving truth that protects us from worry. Meditating on God's Word fills our minds with healthy thoughts. Then the truth we know speaks calmly to silence the anxious thoughts that invade our minds. We often waste valuable time and energy worrying and fretting about things we cannot control. Instead, Paul's challenge is to refocus our attention on God and His ways.

Paul also called us to think about doctrine applied or lived out. The words *pure, lovely,* and *commendable* all speak to actions that overflow from the Spirit's work. It's easy to spend our time concentrating on our own failures or those of others, but we are called to consider that which is pure, lovely, and commendable. It may require turning off the television or putting down the latest gossip magazine, but we gain so much in exchange.

Take a moment right now to consider: What is something true, honorable, and just that you can think about today? What's your favorite scripture? Write it out in the space provided.

Do you know someone living a life that is pure, lovely, and commendable? Take a few moments to write, email, text, or call your friend and share how you see God's work in her life. It will allow you both an opportunity to rejoice in the Lord.

As we spend time considering the ways God is at work, we find ourselves spurred toward peace and gratitude. By choosing prayer, thanksgiving, and praiseworthy thinking, our hearts and minds are changed. God's peace is the midwife that births our joy.

Upside-Down Living

Joy in Giving

Philippians 4:10–23

Contentment is not based upon circumstances. It can't be. Paul and Silas were content in some of the worst circumstances imaginable. . . . Instead of being sourced on the outside and subject to changing circumstances, biblical contentment comes from within and endures through the spectrum of circumstances. How else can we explain the singing that filled the Philippian dungeon?

—Erik Raymond

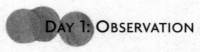

DAY 1: OBSERVATION

What Does the Text Say?

Whether we're on our computers, watching television, or even using a public restroom, advertising surrounds us. Wherever we go, someone is telling us what we need to make our lives better, more enjoyable, or complete. Commercials often stir in us a desire for something we didn't even know we wanted. It could be a product that promises to make our hair shine or a cream to make our skin glow. Or perhaps a new kitchen gadget or office supply that promises we'll work faster and be more productive. Seeing it makes us want it.

It's easy to believe the beautiful woman on the commercial who's telling us that getting more is the pathway to joy. It's even more compelling when a friend or neighbor raves about a new product. Slowly we start to think that if we could just have a little more, our lives would be better.

We all suffer from "keeping up with the Joneses" syndrome at some point in our lives. And our desires go beyond material items, don't they? We see our co-worker's exciting job situation, our neighbor's thoughtful husband, or our friend's natural giftedness and find ourselves wanting a bigger slice of life's proverbial pie. We see so much of the world these days that it's easy to feel like we're missing out.

This week we'll see once again the upside-down nature of the gospel. Our lives aren't filled by collecting the latest and greatest gadgets or trying to be just like everyone else. Our lives are filled as we generously pour them out in service to one another. We gain life not by getting but by giving.

Today we'll begin by reading our last section of the book of Philippians. Open your time in prayer, asking the Lord for insight as you study His Word.

Read **Philippians 4:10–23.**

> [10]I rejoiced in the Lord greatly that now at length you have revived
> your concern for me. You were indeed concerned for me, but you
> had no opportunity. [11]Not that I am speaking of being in need, for I

have learned in whatever situation I am to be content. [12]I know how to be brought low, and I know how to abound. In any and every circumstance, I have learned the secret of facing plenty and hunger, abundance and need. [13]I can do all things through him who strengthens me.

[14]Yet it was kind of you to share my trouble. [15]And you Philippians yourselves know that in the beginning of the gospel, when I left Macedonia, no church entered into partnership with me in giving and receiving, except you only. [16]Even in Thessalonica you sent me help for my needs once and again. [17]Not that I seek the gift, but I seek the fruit that increases to your credit. [18]I have received full payment, and more. I am well supplied, having received from Epaphroditus the gifts you sent, a fragrant offering, a sacrifice acceptable and pleasing to God. [19]And my God will supply every need of yours according to his riches in glory in Christ Jesus. [20]To our God and Father be glory forever and ever. Amen.

[21]Greet every saint in Christ Jesus. The brothers who are with me greet you. [22]All the saints greet you, especially those of Caesar's household.

[23]The grace of the Lord Jesus Christ be with your spirit.

1. What reason did Paul give for why he greatly rejoiced in the Lord?

2. What did he say about his own personal contentment?

3. How was Paul strengthened for any and every circumstance?

4. In what ways had the Philippians given assistance to Paul on prior occasions? How did their generosity compare to the other Macedonian churches?

5. How did Paul describe their gifts (verse 18)?

6. What promise did Paul give them (verse 19)?

7. As Paul closed the letter, what were his final thoughts and greetings?

8. What word did he use to refer to Christians? How is this similar to his original greeting in the opening lines of Philippians?

Paul began his letter by joyfully recounting the partnership in the gospel he shared with the Philippians. Now, at the close of his letter, we learn more about the partnership they shared: it was one of both giving and receiving. Not only did they receive the gospel message from Paul, but they also gave to Paul to support his ministry. Their giving wasn't solely financial. Paul wrote, "It was kind of you to share my trouble." The Philippians cared deeply for Paul, just as Paul cared deeply for them. When Paul was in trouble, they felt it too. They demonstrated a true concern for his welfare. None of the other churches entered into partnership with Paul as the Philippians did.

Often we forget that leaders in the church may need us to share in their troubles. Day after day, pastors, elders, and ministry leaders give advice, support, teaching, and physical care to men, women, teenagers, and children. It's easy to forget they also need to receive care from us.

Take a moment to consider: How could you support, help, or encourage your pastors or ministry leaders in your church this week?

Perhaps you could write a note of thanksgiving for their ministry, bring their families a meal, or send an email asking how you could pray for them. Take some time now to pray for your pastors, Bible study leaders, and any other leaders in your life, asking the Lord to encourage, strengthen, and provide for them as they faithfully serve.

Day 2: Interpretation

What Does the Text Mean?

I hate to admit this, but most of the time when I'm scheduled to speak to a women's group or some other ministry endeavor, I don't look forward to it. An introvert at heart, I would rather stay home, curled up on my couch with a book. Yet every time I go, I come back filled with joy. There's something about pouring out our lives and giving to others that actually gives us life. By contrast, the more I focus on myself, my preferences, and getting what I want, the grouchier and more discontent I tend to be.

We can give to others in a variety of ways. We can give of our money, time, talents, and other resources. Throughout Scripture, God calls us to be cheerful in our giving (2 Corinthians 9:7) and sacrificial in our living (Romans 12:1). For me, giving sacrificially often involves standing up in front of a large group of women and teaching the Bible. For you, it might mean taking the time to counsel a younger woman in your church or helping support a family with financial needs.

Giving isn't always easy. It usually comes at a cost. However, sacrificial giving is a beautiful reflection of our Savior. He paid the ultimate price for our sakes. Our generous giving is also a sign of our faith in God's ability to supply all we need. It involves risk and reliance on the Lord. As we trust in the Lord in new ways, we experience God's provision each and every time. Playing a part in God's work in the world fills us with joy. Few activities are more exciting than building something that will last for eternity.

Today we'll look again at the final verses of Philippians, hoping to understand them more fully. Open your time in prayer, asking for wisdom and insight as you read.

Read **Philippians 4:10–23** on pages 188–89.

1. Why did Paul rejoice in the gift of the Philippians?

2. Think back on the various circumstances in Paul's life. How do you think his experiences helped him learn the secret of contentment both in plenty and in need?

3. Paul stated that he could do "all things through him who strengthens me." Often this verse is quoted on its own, out of context, to suggest we can accomplish whatever we put our minds to. Look back at the entire passage.

   a. What does "all things" refer to in this passage?

   b. How does that shape your understanding of this verse?

4. How can Christians take hold of Christ's power in our lives? What are some means God has given for us to be strengthened in our faith?

5. Paul stated that the Philippians were the only church to share with him in the matter of giving and receiving.

   a. What does their willingness to give financially demonstrate about their faith?

   b. What does their willingness to receive spiritually from Paul demonstrate about their faith?

6. Paul promised that "God will supply every need of yours according to his riches in glory in Christ Jesus." Does this mean God will give us everything we want in this life? What do you think Paul was promising that God will provide?

We often believe happiness comes from gaining more. However, in this passage Paul encouraged the Philippians by recognizing how they had demonstrated faith and courage by giving generously. On multiple occasions they had supported Paul's efforts for the gospel, even when they were alone in their giving.

As we sacrificially give to others, it's tempting to be fearful. We worry that if we offer too much in a particular area, we might not have enough for our own needs. However, according to Paul, faithful giving of our time, resources, abilities, and prayers will not leave us depleted and lacking. He reminded the Philippians (and each of us), "My God will supply every need of yours according to his riches in glory in Christ Jesus."

In order to put off fear in giving, we hold fast to the Lord's promises. Faithful giving demonstrates active trust in God's faithful provision. It takes courage to give generously, both in times of plenty and in times of need.

In seasons of abundance, we're tempted to believe we should save our resources for coming difficulties or use them for our own pleasures. When we're lacking in some way, it's tempting to cling to our resources. Faith allows us to give generously out of whatever God has given, recognizing that it all belongs to Him anyway.

While observing the wealthy placing their gifts into the temple treasury, Jesus took note of a poor widow who offered two small copper coins as her gift. He told His disciples, "This poor widow has put in more than all the others" (Luke 21:3, NIV). While some might measure a gift by its tangible value, Jesus measured the gift by the amount of faith it demonstrated. As we grow in our faith, clinging more and more to Jesus, we'll abound in giving—both in plenty and in need.

Close your time in prayer, asking God to show you the ways you can give generously to those around you. Trust in Him to provide all you need for everything you give.

Day 3: Application

How Does the Text Transform Me?

Do you remember the last time you learned something new? A few years ago I was on vacation with my friend Erica and all our kids. The new favorite toy of the summer was something called a RipStik. (It's like a skateboard that wiggles.) Somehow the children convinced us to try to learn how to ride it.

We began by watching them. We asked questions and got their advice. However, we knew that if we really wanted to learn, we had to actually get on the Rip-Stik and try it out for ourselves.

So we decided to go for it. I put one foot on my son's RipStik and immediately fell off. I asked him some follow-up questions and then tried again. This time I stayed on for approximately one second. More questions. More attempts. Finally, I started to get the hang of it, and by the end of the evening, Erica and I were riding around like teenagers. (I'm still shocked one of us didn't end up in the ER.)

Here's what I learned that night about learning: It's not comfortable. It involves risk. It takes time. And it requires putting new skills into practice.

That's why I find it hopeful when I read Paul's words, "I have *learned* in whatever situation I am to be content." Paul didn't immediately become content when he became a Christian. It took time. He probably had days when he struggled to accept what God was doing in his life. But eventually he learned contentment in all things.

You and I have the opportunity to learn contentment too. The strength Christ provided for Paul is available for us. Contentment may not come all at once, but we can learn it. Today, as you read this passage, begin your time in prayer, asking the Lord to show you how to apply these truths. Pray that He will help you learn the secret of contentment in all things, in whatever circumstances you're facing today.

Turn to pages 188–89 and read **Philippians 4:10–23**.

1. Paul rejoiced in the Philippians' gift because it demonstrated their faith. A natural outpouring of a thankful, joyful heart is a longing to share with others who are in need. In what ways do you give to others in the following areas?

   a. Finances

b. Time

c. Prayers (For whom do you pray regularly?)

d. Talents (In what ways has God gifted you, whether hospitality, organization, teaching, helping, or some other ability?)

2. Now consider the same question with regard to your church. Note the ways you give of your finances, time, prayers, and talents to your church community.

a. Finances

b. Time

c. Prayers (For whom do you pray regularly?)

d. Talents (In what ways has God gifted you, whether hospitality, organization, teaching, helping, or some other ability?)

3. Look back over these lists again. In which area do you sense God leading you to give more generously to others? What would this look like? Be as specific as possible.

4. Describe a time when giving to others filled you with joy.

5. What are some reasons you are reluctant to give?

6. As you have grown in your faith, have you seen your contentment grow? If so, in what ways? If not, why do you think that is? What prevents you from experiencing a deeper contentment?

7. What were the "all things" Paul was talking about when he said, "I can do all things through him who strengthens me"? How have you seen this verse taken out of context?

8. What challenges are you facing today where you need His strength to help you walk in contentment and joy?

9. What are some practical ways you can rely on Christ's strength rather than your own?

10. What is the difference between a need and a want?

11. Paul promised, "God will supply every need of yours according to his riches in glory in Christ Jesus." Spend some time writing out the specific needs you have today and asking God to meet them.

12. The overflow of a contented, joyful heart is a desire to worship God. Paul declared, "To our God and Father be glory forever and ever. Amen." Take some time to list five to ten specific things for which you are thankful today. Give God glory. If you're struggling to be thankful, confess that to Him honestly. His grace is sufficient, and His mercies are new every day.

13. Paul closed his letter saying, "The grace of the Lord Jesus Christ be with your spirit." Think of your friends, family, and other people in your life. How can you encourage them toward knowing and growing in their relationship with Christ?

God's provision is guaranteed. It's difficult to believe sometimes when we're struggling with life's difficulties, isn't it? The first time my lower back went out, I was pregnant with our third child. I leaned over to pick up a towel off the floor, and I felt something slip out of place. I couldn't stand up straight for days. Walking, sitting, standing—everything was painful. Unfortunately, this was the first of what would become a recurring struggle.

I spent years enduring back pain. It always seemed my back would go out at the worst moments, while doing the simplest of tasks. Initially, I found myself frustrated, defeated, and discontent. I hated putting my life on hold each time it happened, but I could barely move because of the pain.

Over time and through much prayer, God taught me to be content in the midst of the pain. That didn't mean the physical discomfort was less severe. However, the inner wrestling about my situation changed. My frustration changed to a calm assurance and acceptance. God gave me an inner peace about my circumstance.

Accepting the pain didn't mean I gave up searching for solutions. I sought my doctor's advice, tried physical therapy, and exercised regularly to bring relief. Contentment doesn't mean we stop seeking solutions to difficult circumstances. Contentment means we trust God as we deal with them.

My back pain allowed me opportunities to trust God in new ways. As I sat on the couch, I prayed and read the Bible. I realized I could faithfully serve others through prayer even when I couldn't make a meal or do my family's laundry.

Eventually, a doctor realized what was wrong, and I've been free of back pain for several years. I'm so thankful. Yet I'm also thankful for learning in a tangible way the sufficiency of Christ's strength in the midst of physical pain.

Martyn Lloyd-Jones suggested the following translation for Philippians 4:13: "I am strong or made strong, for all things in the One who constantly infuses strength into me."[1] Isn't that a beautiful image? Christ infuses us with the strength we need. When we're faint and unable to keep going, He revives our weary hearts. His strength is all sufficient because He is all powerful.

Close your time today in prayer, asking Jesus to infuse you with strength for all that He's given you today.

DAY 4: REVIEW OF PHILIPPIANS

Paul's epistles make clear his strong desire for his readers to grow in their knowledge of God as well as in their desire to glorify God in all things. He regularly taught key truths through his writing. He described God's character: His unrelenting love, His divine power, His unsearchable wisdom, His complete sovereignty, and His eternal goodness. And he explained how God manifested His love for us in our redemption through salvation in Jesus. He wanted us to know who God is and what He's done for us in Christ.

Paul also explained how our understanding of God affects how we live. He didn't want his readers to have merely an intellectual knowledge of God; he expected that a true awareness of God would affect the lives of believers in profound ways. Essentially, faith in God leads to actions that glorify God.

Today we'll spend our lesson reviewing the book of Philippians. We'll read Paul's letter all the way through one more time. Now that you've studied it for nine weeks, I hope these words feel familiar, like sitting down with an old friend. And I hope that as you read it again, you'll see something you didn't notice before. May you hear from God today in a fresh way through Philippians.

As you read each chapter, pause to reflect on two things. First, list the truths Paul wanted his readers to believe about God, Jesus, the gospel, and themselves. Second, list the exhortations or commands Paul gave. How did he expect believers to live in light of the truths he explained?

Open your time in prayer, asking God to guide you as you read.

Turn to pages 221–25 and read **the book of Philippians**.

Chapter 1
Truths to believe

Exhortations to live out

Chapter 2
Truths to believe

Exhortations to live out

Chapter 3
Truths to believe

Exhortations to live out

Chapter 4
Truths to believe

Exhortations to live out

1. As we close our study on Philippians, what truth have you encountered that was most challenging or difficult? Explain your answer.

2. What is one specific exhortation you want to obey or apply to your life in a new way?

3. What verse in Philippians specifically encouraged you? Write down the verse reference so you'll be able to share it with others. Also, write out the verse on an index card and place it where you'll see it every day—by the sink, on your mirror, at your desk—and memorize it over the next week.

Paul closed his letter much as he began. He greeted the saints and sent greetings from the saints. He began with the words "Grace to you," and he ended with "The grace of the Lord Jesus Christ be with your spirit." He reminded believers *who* they are and *what* they've been given.

It's the truth you and I need to hear again and again:

You are a saint. You're a beloved child of God. He chose you before the creation of the world to be holy and blameless in His sight. Nothing can separate you from His love. Your true home is heaven, and He's preparing a place for you where there are no tears, no sighs, no sicknesses.

Why are you a saint? Not because of your own perfection. Not because of your own good works or because you try really hard. You're a saint because of His grace. From beginning to end, His grace is a gift, extended to you because Jesus made a way for you to draw near to

God. His perfect life, His willing sacrifice, His miraculous resurrection—all are grace to you. He had you in mind when He purchased your redemption. For the joy set before Him, He endured the cross. His grace is sufficient for your salvation, and His grace empowers you to walk in a manner worthy of the gospel. Daily He infuses you with more grace so you can do all things through Jesus who strengthens you.

Do you hear the good news of who you are and what you've been given? You're a grace-filled saint who has every reason to rejoice.

May God impress these truths on your heart. Say them to yourself over and over. Believe. And let them propel you to unshakeable joy in all things.

"Rejoice in the Lord always; again I will say, rejoice!"

DAY 5: DEVOTIONAL

Jesus Cares About Your Joy

These things I have spoken to you, that my joy may be in you, and that your joy may be full.

—JOHN 15:11

Last words matter. When someone dies, we often think back to our final conversation, remembering and reflecting on what we said to each other. I hope my final words will be full of love and care for those I leave behind.

On the night before He died, Jesus shared a final meal and conversation with His disciples. Though they didn't understand that Jesus was about to die, Jesus knew His time was short. What was Jesus concerned about as He prepared to leave those He loved?

The apostle John recorded much of their conversation. In John 14–16 we read that Jesus comforted His disciples and encouraged them to not be troubled. He assured them that although He was going away, He would come back for them. He told them that if they loved Him, they would obey Him. He explained that the Spirit would come and dwell within them and be with them always.

He also taught them to abide. He told them He was the Vine and they were the branches. Apart from Jesus they could do nothing. They'd be dry and useless. But if they would abide in His Word and in prayer and obey His commandments, they would bear much fruit—all to the glory of God.

And then Jesus explained *why* He was telling them all these things. His answer is somewhat surprising. We get so caught up in what we're supposed to do that we often forget the reason Jesus wants us to do what He's asking.

As Jesus spoke these words, He was on His way to the cross. He was preparing to endure unimaginable pain. At this moment, what was on His mind? What goal prompted His last words to those He loved?

"These things I have spoken to you, that my joy may be in you, and that your joy may be full" (John 15:11).

Jesus was concerned about our joy.

As I write these words right now, my eyes brim with tears. Love so amazing, so divine! At the height of His own agony, His love desired my joy and yours. It's unbelievable, isn't it? For the joy set before Him, Jesus endured the cross (Hebrews 12:2).

And Jesus wasn't hoping for us to have a little bit of happiness. He wants us to have fullness of joy—overflowing, abundant. Our joy matters to Jesus.

Here's what Jesus knows: He knows that joy isn't found in the latest and greatest new gadget. It's not found in getting our way or having more money, more friends, or more adventures.

Jesus is the source of our joy, and He's the sustainer of it. Apart from Him, our lives are made up of empty, meaningless attempts to find satisfaction. We wander, desperately thirsty until we drink from Him. He's the beginning and the end, the Alpha and the Omega. Every good gift is from His hand, and nothing good exists apart from Him. Our desire for joy is ultimately a desire for Jesus.

In our study of Philippians, we've had the opportunity to see genuine joy. Joy begins with salvation and increases as we experience true fellowship, understand Christ's lordship, partake in Christ's humility, and obey God's Word. As we grow in faith, our desires change. We long to know Jesus. We place our hope in heavenly joys rather than earthly circumstances. We pray with thanksgiving rather than fret with anxiety. We give generously to further the work of the gospel.

Just as Paul learned the secret of being content in plenty and in need, as we grow in our dependence on God, we bloom into women of joy. By relying on God, we grow in courage, saying with Paul, "I can do everything through him who gives me strength" (NIV).

We've walked together in this study for nine weeks. I'm so thankful—it's been a joy for me to work through Philippians with you. I hope it's been a fruitful time of study for you as well.

My final words to you reflect my deepest desire for you: Don't stop studying God's Word. Abide in God, pray to Him, seek Him continually.

May His joy be in you, and may it be full.

Study Guide

If you plan to use this study with a group, you may find the following questions helpful in guiding your time together. In most studies I've led, at least a few participants struggle to complete the homework each week. With this in mind, I've tried to arrange these questions to encourage participation from all group members, regardless of whether or not they've finished the lesson.

For each week, I've included both an icebreaker question and an opening question. The icebreaker is just a fun get-to-know-you prompt that allows every woman in the group an opportunity to share. Depending on the size of your group, it may be helpful also to say your names every week during this time. I have found this encourages everyone to speak, even if just to share a little bit about herself. If you have a talkative group, you may need to give them a friendly reminder to keep their answers brief. I've tried to coordinate the icebreaker questions to go along with the lessons in some way, but feel free to use your own or eliminate them altogether if they don't work with your group dynamics.

The opening question is typically broad in order to get the group thinking about the topic of that week's lesson. Unlike the icebreaker, not every participant needs to answer this one, but it does serve as a warm-up before you jump into the deeper study.

The remaining questions are based on the Bible passages studied that week. I've narrowed down the verses and questions covered to accommodate the limitations of your group time.

In most groups there will be pauses in the discussion as the participants take some time to reflect. As a leader my impulse sometimes is to fill the silences or answer the question myself. However, I've come to realize that those moments of silence feel longer to me as the leader than to the members of the group. Allowing everyone time to process a question will help your group share more openly. If no one responds, it may help to reword the question, but feel free to let questions sit for a few moments first. Sometimes I take a sip of coffee after asking a question so I will remember to wait patiently as they process their response.

My greatest encouragement for you as a leader is to pray regularly for your group. Each woman in your study faces struggles you may not know about. How thankful I am that the Lord knows and is working through His Spirit to allow the different passages to speak to each participant in a particular way. Pray that His Spirit will guide your discussion and refresh the women in your group. He promises, "So is my word that goes out from my mouth: It will not return to me empty, but will accomplish what I desire and achieve the purpose for which I sent it" (Isaiah 55:11, NIV).

May God encourage and bless you as you faithfully lead!

WEEK 1: WE NEED MORE THAN A SPIRITUAL EXPERIENCE
Joy in Salvation—Acts 7–16

Icebreaker: What's a small thing that brings you joy? (It could be a favorite smell, a favorite food, a person . . . just something that brings delight to your day.)

Opening Question: Can you describe for us a time when someone came to your rescue?

1. From your reading this week, what did you learn about Paul's life before he became a Christian? See Acts 8:1–3 if needed.
2. How did Paul become a Christian? What plan did God have for Paul's ministry? How did the other disciples feel about Paul? See Acts 9:15, 20 if needed.

Read **Acts 16:9–34.**
3. We find three stories in this passage: Lydia, the slave girl, and the Roman jailer. In each of these stories, how do we see God's pursuit of the person?
4. Can you describe a time when you experienced God's pursuit? Or maybe, like Lydia, you felt the Lord open your heart to respond to the message?

5. In each of these stories, how do we see faith accompanied by action? How did each person's life change after he or she came to faith?

6. What does it mean to believe in Jesus? How does a person become a believer?

7. How have you seen your faith lead you to make different choices? Or can you tell about how you've seen someone's faith change his or her life?

8. What is baptism? Why is it important for Christians?

9. Do you notice any similarities or differences as you look at these Philippian believers? What are their life situations?

10. Acts 16:34 says of the Philippian jailer that "he was filled with joy because he had come to believe in God" (NIV). Why should our salvation bring us joy? Why do you think it sometimes doesn't bring us joy on a daily basis?

11. What is the difference between salvation and a spiritual experience?

12. How do you see people looking for joy in spiritual experiences rather than salvation in the world today?

13. What stood out to you in this particular passage, or what verse encouraged you this week?

Close your time by praying for one another.

Week 2: A Shared Joy

Joy in True Fellowship—Philippians 1:1–11

Icebreaker: What's one characteristic of friendship that is important to you?

Opening Question: What impact have your friendships had on your life—either for good or bad?

Read **Philippians 1:1–11.**

1. Paul explained that he and Timothy were together, writing the letter. He addressed the Philippians by the term *saints.*

a. When you hear the term *saints,* what images are brought to mind?

b. Do you consider yourself a saint? Why or why not?

c. What is the difference between a saint who struggles with sin and a sinner who is working hard to be a saint?

2. Paul recounted his thankfulness for the Philippians because of their partnership in the gospel. Why do you think this type of partnership gave Paul joy? How is it different from friendships linked by other circumstances?

3. What differences have you noticed between friendships with people who share your commitment to Jesus and friendships with those who don't? Can you describe a time when deep intimacy came from doing ministry with someone?

4. What does it look like to be a friend who brings joy and thanksgiving to others? In contrast, how can one be self-seeking in friendship?

5. We looked at some verses that describe various benefits of friendship and others that describe warnings in friendship on pages 44–46. Which of these benefits or warnings stood out to you, and why?

6. Looking back over this passage, what words or phrases describe Paul's feelings toward the Philippians?

7. How did Paul pray for the Philippians? List the different ways he prayed for them. How does his prayer compare or contrast with your prayers for others?

8. How does prayer unify us with others, even when they are far away? Tell about a time when God used prayer to grow your friendship with someone.

9. As you read this passage this week, what did you learn about God? About yourself?

10. What stood out to you in this particular passage, or what verse encouraged you this week?

Close your time by praying for one another.

WEEK 3: UNSHAKEABLE

Joy in Christ's Lordship—Philippians 1:12–30

Icebreaker: What's one attribute or talent you wish you had but clearly isn't part of God's plan for you? (For instance, I wish I could sing, but it's clear that's not God's plan for me!)

Opening Question: What are some ways we live as if we were in control of the universe? How does it wear us out to live that way?

Read **Philippians 1:12–30.**

1. How did Paul view what had happened to him? What was the result of his suffering?

2. As a result of Paul's imprisonment, why would most of the brothers be bolder to speak about Christ without fear? Wouldn't you expect Paul's imprisonment to make them *more* fearful?

3. Why do you think it encourages others to stand firm in their own faith when someone suffers for being a Christian? Can you think of someone who has encouraged your faith by suffering as a Christian?

4. Although Paul faced imprisonment and suffering for preaching Christ, he still preached the message. What concerns prevent us from sharing the gospel with non-Christians in our lives?

5. Why would someone preach Christ because of envy and rivalry? What do you think he or she might be hoping to gain?

6. Paul's outward circumstances were unfavorable. How would you describe his inward condition? What clues in the text point to your conclusions?

7. How have you seen blessings come from suffering in your own life? How has suffering drawn you closer to God or allowed you to help others who are suffering?

8. How did Paul's understanding of his life change his perspective on death?

9. How would the belief that God was in control of their suffering allow the Philippians to stand firm and walk well through it? How would it keep them from fear?

10. What is difficult or confusing for you as you think about Christ's lordship? What about it is comforting to you?

11. How does a belief that God is working all things for good allow you to trust Him? How does it enable you to walk in a manner worthy of the gospel?

12. Have you ever seen anyone you would describe as a "spectacle of glory" in the midst of suffering? Why would you describe him or her that way?

13. What stood out to you in this particular passage, or what verse encouraged you this week?

Close your time by praying for one another.

WEEK 4: THE MORE OF BECOMING LESS

Joy in Humility—Philippians 2:1–11

Icebreaker: What's one of your most embarrassing or humiliating moments?

Opening Question: Where do you see a desire for self-promotion in the world today? What are some of the things we tend to take pride in?

Read **Philippians 2:1–11**.

1. In verse 1 Paul wrote about our union with Christ. If we are "in Christ," he said, certain things will be true of us. What are these five things? How do they result from being unified with Christ?

2. How does being unified with Christ unify us with other people?

3. Why should we be humble as we think of ourselves? Read 1 Corinthians 4:7. How is this true of all of us?

4. I find that my self-focus often springs up in the areas where I'm tempted to compare myself with others. In what ways do women tend

to compare themselves to one another? How does this affect our attitudes and relationships? How can this lead to pride? What would give us humility?

5. Paul urged his readers to have the "same mind" and "same love." Does this mean our service in the body will all look the same? Read Romans 12:3–8. What are some ways we have both unity in Christ and individuality?

6. How do selfish ambition and conceit tear apart unity with others? How does humility foster unity?

7. This week you looked up multiple verses on Christ's life: His birth, ministry, teaching, friendships, and death. How did He display humility in all these areas?

8. What did you learn from Christ's example of humility that we studied this week (His birth, friendships, ministry, suffering, and death)? How would it look for you to follow His example in how you love others?

9. In a "selfie" and "notice me" kind of world, how can we live with humility? What would that look like on a daily basis in contrast to what our culture expects?

10. The paraphrase of Timothy Keller says, "The essence of gospel-humility is not thinking more of myself or thinking less of myself; it is thinking of myself less." What are the ways we spend time thinking about ourselves throughout the day? How would changing what we think about change how we live?

11. What stood out to you in this particular passage, or what verse encouraged you this week?

Close your time by praying for one another.

WEEK 5: WITH HEARTS SET FREE

Joy in Obedience—Philippians 2:12–30

Icebreaker: If you could be in charge of the world for a day, what's one rule you'd make everyone obey or one pet peeve you'd outlaw?

Opening Question: What benefits do we reap from obedience to God? Why do we choose not to obey?

Read **Philippians 2:12–30.**

1. Reread verse 12. What could be potentially confusing about this verse?
2. Based on the verses you read this week, why should we fear the Lord?
3. What does it look like to fear God? How does a person who fears God live in contrast to one who does not?
4. Read Proverbs 2:1–6. How can we grow in a right fear of the Lord?
5. How is a person saved? See 2 Timothy 1:8–9; Ephesians 2:8–10; Romans 10:9–13; 1 John 2:3–6. Based on these verses, how would you answer the following questions?
   a. What role does God play in salvation?
   b. What is our role in salvation?
   c. What role do our works have in salvation?
6. What attitude did Paul tell the Philippians to bring to their obedience? Why does it matter?
7. When are you most tempted to grumble and complain about the call to obedience?
8. How is disobedience a sign of unbelief or distrust in God?
9. Describe a time when obedience to God brought joy even though it involved sacrifice.
10. What did you learn from the examples of Timothy and Epaphroditus? How was their faith displayed in their lives?
11. What stood out to you in this particular passage, or what verse encouraged you this week?

Close your time by praying for one another.

WEEK 6: A FRIEND LIKE NO OTHER

Joy in Knowing Christ—Philippians 3:1–11

Icebreaker: What is something you are naturally good at?

Opening Question: What aspects of our backgrounds are we tempted to take pride in?

Read **Philippians 3:1–11.**

1. What command did Paul give in verse 1? What's the difference between rejoicing in the Lord and rejoicing in our circumstances?

2. What characteristic of God helps you rejoice when you don't feel joyful? Share a verse that gives you hope in difficult times.

3. Why did Paul say that rejoicing in the Lord is "safe" for us? What does giving thanks protect us from? How have you experienced this?

4. Whom did Paul describe as "dogs" and "mutilators of the flesh" (verse 2, NIV)? Why did he warn against them?

5. From your reading this week, what did Paul mean by *circumcision*? With whom was it established and for what purpose?

6. What's the difference between circumcision of the flesh and circumcision of the heart? See Deuteronomy 10:15–21; 30:4–10; Romans 2:28–29; Galatians 6:12–16.

7. In what current church rituals do some people place their confidence, while neglecting a true relationship with God? How is this detrimental to one's own faith as well as harmful to the church?

8. What reasons did Paul have for boasting? In what areas are we, like Paul, tempted to put "confidence in the flesh"?

9. What is legalism? How does that compare with joyful obedience to God?

10. How does legalism extinguish joy? How does attempting to live up to a standard each day (even our own) leave us weary and exhausted?

11. In what circumstances are you most often tempted to trust in your own abilities rather than rely on Christ?

12. How does what we desire determine how we live?

13. How can we seek to know Christ in new ways?

14. What stood out to you in this particular passage, or what verse encouraged you this week?

Close your time by praying for one another.

WEEK 7: SOMETHING BETTER IS COMING

Joy in Heaven—Philippians 3:12–4:1

Icebreaker: What is the farthest place you've traveled to?

Opening Question: Can you tell about a time or place when you felt you didn't belong? How did this affect your behavior?

Read **Philippians 3:12–4:1**.

1. Paul stated, "Not that I have already obtained *this*." Read back over the passage from last week for context. What had he not yet obtained?

2. Why is it helpful to know that Paul had not yet obtained perfection? How does that encourage you?

3. Paul soberly considered himself and chose to forget what lay behind him. How can reliving and reviewing our past inhibit spiritual growth? Consider the impact of both a prideful view of past accomplishments and a shameful view of past failures.

4. Paul used the phrase "straining forward to what lies ahead." What would it look like to strain toward being like Jesus?

5. Why did Paul command his readers to live up to what they had already attained? What is dangerous about apathy when it comes to faith?

6. What does it mean to live as an enemy of the cross of Christ?

7. How does sin lead to destruction in our lives?

8. What are some ways the world encourages us to satisfy our cravings and to glory in shame?

9. Have you ever been affected by false teachings? What impact did they have on your faith?

10. How does having our minds set on earthly things rob us of joy?

11. How are your expectations when traveling different than when you are at home? How can we apply that principle to our lives on earth? How does knowing your citizenship is in heaven help you to live differently? (See 1 Peter 2:11.)

12. C. S. Lewis observed, "Aim at Heaven and you will get earth 'thrown in': aim at earth and you get neither." How have you seen this principle proven true in your own life?

13. What stood out to you in this particular passage, or what verse encouraged you this week?

Close your time by praying for one another.

WEEK 8: A HEART AT PEACE

Joy in the Inner Life—Philippians 4:2–9

Icebreaker: Name something that causes you fear or anxiety (for example, heights, spiders, flying, syrup touching your bacon).

Opening Question: When you think about the word *peace,* what comes to mind? How do people typically go about seeking peace in their lives?

Read **Philippians 4:2–9.**

1. Why would Paul be concerned for Euodia and Syntyche to agree with each other in the Lord? How would disunity among leaders in the church affect the church body?

2. What's the difference between disagreements over disputable matters and disagreements over important doctrines of the church? See Romans 14:1–4 and Galatians 5:16–21.

3. What would it look like for us to work toward unity with someone when we disagree over a disputable matter?

4. What are some causes of anxiety in our world today?

5. According to this passage, what are we supposed to do with our concerns? Why is this so difficult?

6. How can we cultivate habits of prayer in our daily lives? What has helped you in this regard?

7. What do you think it means that "the peace of God . . . will guard your hearts"? Can you describe an occasion when you experienced an unexplainable sense of peace in a difficult time?

8. What are ways we feed our minds as we go through the day? How does what we see, read, and hear affect what we think about?

9. What are ways to fill our minds with true and praiseworthy thoughts?

10. What is the danger of not putting into action what we know to be true?

11. Who has been an example for you of what it means to be a Christian? What about his or her example helped to grow your faith?

12. What stood out to you in this particular passage, or what verse encouraged you this week?

Close your time by praying for one another.

WEEK 9: UPSIDE-DOWN LIVING

Joy in Giving—Philippians 4:10–23

Icebreaker: What's a favorite gift you've either given or received?

Opening Question: If you could describe a visual image of contentment, what would it look like?

Read **Philippians 4:10–23**.

1. How do you think Paul learned the secret of contentment in whatever circumstance he faced? Why do you think he could declare with such assurance that he had learned contentment?

2. Are there ever right reasons to be discontent? If so, what would they be? If not, why not?

3. What temptations do we face when we are in short supply of something? What temptations do we face when we have plenty?

4. What are some places we seek contentment apart from Jesus? How have you seen those items fail to satisfy?

5. Paul stated that he could do "all things through him who strengthens me." How can Christians take hold of Christ's strength? What are some means He has given us to take hold of His power?

6. As you have grown in your faith, have you seen your contentment grow? Explain your answer.

7. Paul rejoiced in the Philippians' giving because it said something about their faith. A natural outpouring of a thankful, joyful heart is a longing to share with others in need. In what area would you most like to grow in the grace of giving? Financially? Using your time for others? Prayer? Using your gifts to help others?

8. How have you been blessed by someone's giving to you? How did his or her generosity affect you, and how did it shape your perspective on giving?

9. What should our attitude be as we give? Why?

10. Why does it take courage to give sacrificially?

11. As you think back over the book of Philippians, what specific verse most influenced you? Why did you choose that verse?

12. Jesus is concerned about your joy. (See John 15:11.) How does that encourage you?

13. What stood out to you in this particular passage, or what verse encouraged you this week?

Close your time by praying for one another.

The Book of Philippians

Chapter 1

[1] Paul and Timothy, servants of Christ Jesus,

To all the saints in Christ Jesus who are at Philippi, with the overseers and deacons:

[2] Grace to you and peace from God our Father and the Lord Jesus Christ.

[3] I thank my God in all my remembrance of you, [4] always in every prayer of mine for you all making my prayer with joy, [5] because of your partnership in the gospel from the first day until now. [6] And I am sure of this, that he who began a good work in you will bring it to completion at the day of Jesus Christ. [7] It is right for me to feel this way about you all, because I hold you in my heart, for you are all partakers with me of grace, both in my imprisonment and in the defense and confirmation of the gospel. [8] For God is my witness, how I yearn for you all with the affection of Christ Jesus. [9] And it is my prayer that your love may abound more and more, with knowledge and all discernment, [10] so that you may approve what is excellent, and so be pure and blameless for the day of Christ, [11] filled with the fruit of righteousness that comes through Jesus Christ, to the glory and praise of God.

[12] I want you to know, brothers, that what has happened to me has really served to advance the gospel, [13] so that it has become known throughout the whole imperial guard and to all the rest that my imprisonment is for Christ. [14] And most of the brothers, having become confident in the Lord by my imprisonment, are much more bold to speak the word without fear.

[15] Some indeed preach Christ from envy and rivalry, but others from good will. [16] The latter do it out of love, knowing that I am put here for the defense of the gospel. [17] The former proclaim Christ out of selfish ambition, not sincerely but thinking to afflict me in my imprisonment. [18] What then? Only that in every way, whether in pretense or in truth, Christ is proclaimed, and in that I rejoice.

Yes, and I will rejoice, [19] for I know that through your prayers and the help of the Spirit of Jesus Christ this will turn out for my deliverance, [20] as it is my eager expectation and hope that I will not be at all ashamed, but that with full courage now as always Christ will be honored in my body, whether by life or by death. ²¹ For to me to live is Christ, and to die is gain. ²² If I am to live in the flesh, that means fruitful labor for me. Yet which I shall choose I cannot tell. ²³ I am hard pressed between the two. My desire is to depart and be with Christ, for that is far better. ²⁴ But to remain in the flesh is more necessary on your account. ²⁵ Convinced of this, I know that I will remain and continue with you all, for your progress and joy in the faith, ²⁶ so that in me you may have ample cause to glory in Christ Jesus, because of my coming to you again.

²⁷ Only let your manner of life be worthy of the gospel of Christ, so that whether I come and see you or am absent, I may hear of you that you are standing firm in one spirit, with one mind striving side by side for the faith of the gospel, ²⁸ and not frightened in anything by your opponents. This is a clear sign to them of their destruction, but of your salvation, and that from God. ²⁹ For it has been granted to you that for the sake of Christ you should not only believe in him but also suffer for his sake, ³⁰ engaged in the same conflict that you saw I had and now hear that I still have.

Chapter 2

¹ So if there is any encouragement in Christ, any comfort from love, any participation in the Spirit, any affection and sympathy, ² complete my joy by being of the same mind, having the same love, being in full accord and of one mind. ³ Do nothing from selfish ambition or conceit, but in humility count others more significant than yourselves. ⁴ Let each of you look not only to his own interests, but also to the interests of others. ⁵ Have this mind among yourselves, which is yours in Christ Jesus, ⁶ who, though he was in the form of God, did not count equality with God a thing to be grasped, ⁷ but emptied himself, by taking the form of a servant, being born in the likeness of men. ⁸ And being found in human form, he humbled himself by becoming obedient to the point of death, even death on a cross. ⁹ Therefore God has highly exalted him and bestowed on him the name that is above every name, ¹⁰ so that at the name of Jesus every knee should bow, in heaven and on earth and under the earth, ¹¹ and every tongue confess that Jesus Christ is Lord, to the glory of God the Father.

¹² Therefore, my beloved, as you have always obeyed, so now, not only as in my

presence but much more in my absence, work out your own salvation with fear and trembling, ¹³for it is God who works in you, both to will and to work for his good pleasure.

¹⁴Do all things without grumbling or disputing, ¹⁵that you may be blameless and innocent, children of God without blemish in the midst of a crooked and twisted generation, among whom you shine as lights in the world, ¹⁶holding fast to the word of life, so that in the day of Christ I may be proud that I did not run in vain or labor in vain. ¹⁷Even if I am to be poured out as a drink offering upon the sacrificial offering of your faith, I am glad and rejoice with you all. ¹⁸Likewise you also should be glad and rejoice with me.

¹⁹I hope in the Lord Jesus to send Timothy to you soon, so that I too may be cheered by news of you. ²⁰For I have no one like him, who will be genuinely concerned for your welfare. ²¹For they all seek their own interests, not those of Jesus Christ. ²²But you know Timothy's proven worth, how as a son with a father he has served with me in the gospel. ²³I hope therefore to send him just as soon as I see how it will go with me, ²⁴and I trust in the Lord that shortly I myself will come also.

²⁵I have thought it necessary to send to you Epaphroditus my brother and fellow worker and fellow soldier, and your messenger and minister to my need, ²⁶for he has been longing for you all and has been distressed because you heard that he was ill. ²⁷Indeed he was ill, near to death. But God had mercy on him, and not only on him but on me also, lest I should have sorrow upon sorrow. ²⁸I am the more eager to send him, therefore, that you may rejoice at seeing him again, and that I may be less anxious. ²⁹So receive him in the Lord with all joy, and honor such men, ³⁰for he nearly died for the work of Christ, risking his life to complete what was lacking in your service to me.

Chapter 3

¹Finally, my brothers, rejoice in the Lord. To write the same things to you is no trouble to me and is safe for you.

²Look out for the dogs, look out for the evildoers, look out for those who mutilate the flesh. ³For we are the circumcision, who worship by the Spirit of God and glory in Christ Jesus and put no confidence in the flesh—⁴though I myself have reason for confidence in the flesh also. If anyone else thinks he has reason for confidence in the flesh, I have more: ⁵circumcised on the eighth day, of the people of

Israel, of the tribe of Benjamin, a Hebrew of Hebrews; as to the law, a Pharisee; [6]as to zeal, a persecutor of the church; as to righteousness under the law, blameless. [7]But whatever gain I had, I counted as loss for the sake of Christ. [8]Indeed, I count everything as loss because of the surpassing worth of knowing Christ Jesus my Lord. For his sake I have suffered the loss of all things and count them as rubbish, in order that I may gain Christ [9]and be found in him, not having a righteousness of my own that comes from the law, but that which comes through faith in Christ, the righteousness from God that depends on faith—[10]that I may know him and the power of his resurrection, and may share his sufferings, becoming like him in his death, [11]that by any means possible I may attain the resurrection from the dead.

[12]Not that I have already obtained this or am already perfect, but I press on to make it my own, because Christ Jesus has made me his own. [13]Brothers, I do not consider that I have made it my own. But one thing I do: forgetting what lies behind and straining forward to what lies ahead, [14]I press on toward the goal for the prize of the upward call of God in Christ Jesus. [15]Let those of us who are mature think this way, and if in anything you think otherwise, God will reveal that also to you.[16]Only let us hold true to what we have attained.

[17]Brothers, join in imitating me, and keep your eyes on those who walk according to the example you have in us. [18]For many, of whom I have often told you and now tell you even with tears, walk as enemies of the cross of Christ. [19]Their end is destruction, their god is their belly, and they glory in their shame, with minds set on earthly things. [20]But our citizenship is in heaven, and from it we await a Savior, the Lord Jesus Christ, [21]who will transform our lowly body to be like his glorious body, by the power that enables him even to subject all things to himself.

Chapter 4

[1]Therefore, my brothers, whom I love and long for, my joy and crown, stand firm thus in the Lord, my beloved.

[2]I entreat Euodia and I entreat Syntyche to agree in the Lord. [3]Yes, I ask you also, true companion, help these women, who have labored side by side with me in the gospel together with Clement and the rest of my fellow workers, whose names are in the book of life.

[4]Rejoice in the Lord always; again I will say, rejoice. [5]Let your reasonableness be known to everyone. The Lord is at hand; [6]do not be anxious about anything,

but in everything by prayer and supplication with thanksgiving let your requests be made known to God. [7]And the peace of God, which surpasses all understanding, will guard your hearts and your minds in Christ Jesus.

[8]Finally, brothers, whatever is true, whatever is honorable, whatever is just, whatever is pure, whatever is lovely, whatever is commendable, if there is any excellence, if there is anything worthy of praise, think about these things. [9]What you have learned and received and heard and seen in me—practice these things, and the God of peace will be with you.

[10]I rejoiced in the Lord greatly that now at length you have revived your concern for me. You were indeed concerned for me, but you had no opportunity. [11]Not that I am speaking of being in need, for I have learned in whatever situation I am to be content. [12]I know how to be brought low, and I know how to abound. In any and every circumstance, I have learned the secret of facing plenty and hunger, abundance and need. [13]I can do all things through him who strengthens me.

[14]Yet it was kind of you to share my trouble. [15]And you Philippians yourselves know that in the beginning of the gospel, when I left Macedonia, no church entered into partnership with me in giving and receiving, except you only. [16]Even in Thessalonica you sent me help for my needs once and again. [17]Not that I seek the gift, but I seek the fruit that increases to your credit. [18]I have received full payment, and more. I am well supplied, having received from Epaphroditus the gifts you sent, a fragrant offering, a sacrifice acceptable and pleasing to God.[19]And my God will supply every need of yours according to his riches in glory in Christ Jesus. [20]To our God and Father be glory forever and ever. Amen.

[21]Greet every saint in Christ Jesus. The brothers who are with me greet you. [22]All the saints greet you, especially those of Caesar's household.

[23]The grace of the Lord Jesus Christ be with your spirit.

Acknowledgments

As I finish this book, I am thankful. The Lord has met me in tender ways along this journey and once again shown me that He is able to do immeasurably more than all I ask or imagine.

The Lord provided encouraging friends to walk alongside me. Megan Hill, Winfree Brisley, Catriona Anderson, and Ashley Mink read as I wrote and offered encouraging feedback and helpful editing advice. Behind the scenes were the faithful prayers and words of support of Susan Foster, Trillia Newbell, Wallace Barnes, Courtney Reissig, Anne Rogers, Chris Vaughn, Erica Crumpler, Tracy Thornton, Kate Willis, Lisa Marie Ferguson, Kimberly Curlin, Peggy Chapman, Macon Collins, Angela Queen, Dottie Bryan, Heather Jones, Lisa Cosper, Anne Abner, and Beth Herring. I treasure your friendship and needed every one of your prayers!

I have the privilege to work alongside excellent editors and gifted writers at the Gospel Coalition. Thank you, Collin Hansen and Matt Smethurst, for encouraging my writing (and making it better) and for the entire team praying for me in this project. Additionally, I'm thankful for the support of Tom and Ann Hawkes, my fellow staff members at Uptown Church, and our Women's Care Team. It is a joy to work with you all, particularly my women's ministry partner, Lauren Palmer— she has been such a gift to me! Also, it's a privilege to be a part of the Reformed Theological Seminary family. They have cheered me on (especially our chancellor, Ligon Duncan) and provided excellent resources that helped in the writing of this book.

I am indebted to both Robert Wolgemuth and Austin Wilson for their helpful assistance and advice. They handle all the details of the publishing process so well and give me the freedom to focus on writing. Thank you for all you do.

The entire Multnomah team is a delight. In particular, this book is so much better in every way because of my editor, Laura Barker. Her friendship, encouragement, and editing wisdom are invaluable. I can't say "thank you" enough for all her help with and excitement about this book.

Neil, Sydney, and Aidan Chapman graciously allowed me to share parts of

Debbie's story in this book. When we studied Philippians together years ago, Debbie was a true example of contentment in all things. Reading through our old emails brought me to tears so many times—I miss her. I'm thankful to get to share her words and faithfulness with others.

My family was incredibly supportive while I was working on this project. My parents, Bob and Anita Bryan, cheer me on in everything I do. My children—Emma, John, and Kate—bring daily joy and laughter into my life. They prayed for me, wrote loving notes, and cheerfully let me spend Saturdays writing. I promise we'll have more "scone Saturdays" now that this project is finished.

I couldn't do any of the writing I do without the support of my husband, Mike. He prays for me, helps me find time to write, and patiently answers all the theological and biblical questions I regularly send his way. (It's pretty great to live with a New Testament professor when you're writing on Philippians.) We celebrated twenty years of marriage this summer, and I've never been more thankful to be his wife.

My friend Shanna Davis is the reason this book came to be written. We may live far away from each other, but Jesus unites our hearts in a shared mission, passion, joy, and eternal home we're looking forward to. I love our long conversations that often overflow in tears, our fun days by the pool each summer, and our shared partnership in the gospel. She's a light for the gospel everywhere she goes.

And to my readers: thank you. So many of you have written me letters of encouragement after reading *Walking with God in the Season of Motherhood*. Often the notes came to my inbox just when I was feeling discouraged or didn't particularly feel like writing. Thank you for reminding me why I write.

My prayer for us all: "May the God of hope fill you with all joy and peace in believing, so that by the power of the Holy Spirit you may abound in hope" (Romans 15:13).

Notes

Introduction: An Invitation to Joy

1. *Sermons of Samuel Ward* (Edinburgh, Scotland: Banner of Truth, 1996), 25–27, quoted in Richard Rushing, ed., *Voices from the Past: Puritan Devotional Readings* (Edinburgh, Scotland: Banner of Truth, 2009), 47.

Week 1: We Need More Than a Spiritual Experience

The epigraph is taken from Martyn Lloyd-Jones, *The Life of Joy: A Commentary on Philippians 1 and 2* (Grand Rapids, MI: Baker, 1989), 15.

1. Matthew Mead, *A Name in Heaven the Truest Ground of Joy* (Morgan, PA: Soli Deo Gloria, 1996), 19–38, quoted in Richard Rushing, ed., *Voices from the Past: Puritan Devotional Readings* (Edinburgh, Scotland: Banner of Truth, 2009), 277.

Week 2: A Shared Joy

The epigraph is taken from *The Beloved Works of C. S. Lewis: Surprised by Joy, Reflections on the Psalms, The Four Loves, The Business of Heaven* (New York: Inspirational, 1998), 261.

1. John Blanchard as quoted in Donald S. Whitney, *Spiritual Disciplines for the Christian Life* (Colorado Springs: NavPress, 1991), 33.
2. *Apple Dictionary,* Version 2.2.1, s.v. "peace."
3. *Beloved Works,* 249.
4. L. M. Montgomery, *Anne of Green Gables* (New York: Harper Collins, 1908), 58.

Week 3: Unshakeable

The epigraph is taken from J. I. Packer, *Concise Theology: A Guide to Historic Christian Beliefs* (Wheaton, IL: Tyndale, 1993), 56.

1. Thomas Watson, *The Art of Divine Contentment* (Hollis, NH: Puritan, 2009), 57.

2. Joni Eareckson Tada, "Finding Jesus in Your Gethsemane," interview by Betsy Childs Howard, The Gospel Coalition, podcast, December 2, 2016, www.thegospelcoalition.org/article/joni-eareckson-tada-on-finding-jesus -in-your-gethsemane/.

3. John M. Frame, *The Doctrine of God: A Theology of Lordship* (Phillipsburg, NJ: P and R Publishing, 2002), 59.

4. The Belgic Confession (1561), article 13 "Of Divine Providence," Ligonier Ministries, www.ligonier.org/learn/articles/belgic-confession-1561/.

5. Thomas à Kempis, *The Imitation of Christ* (London: Fontana Books, 1963), 134.

Week 4: The More of Becoming Less

The epigraph is taken from Thomas Brooks, *Precious Remedies Against Satan's Devices* (Lexington, KY: Feather Trail, 2010), 156.

1. Frank Houghton, "Thou Who Wast Rich Beyond All Splendor," copyright © 1934, OMF International.

2. Timothy Keller, *The Freedom of Self-Forgetfulness: The Path to True Christian Joy* (Leyland, UK: 10Publishing, 2012), 36.

3. Hannah Anderson, *Humble Roots: How Humility Grounds and Nourishes Your Soul* (Chicago: Moody, 2016), 57.

4. Andrew Johnson and Andy McSmith, "Children Say Being Famous Is Best Thing in World," *Independent,* December 18, 2006, www.independent.co .uk/news/uk/this-britain/children-say-being-famous-is-best-thing-in-world -5331661.html.

Week 5: With Hearts Set Free

The epigraph is taken from Martyn Lloyd-Jones, *The Life of Joy: A Commentary on Philippians 1 and 2* (Grand Rapids, MI: Baker, 1989), 178.

1. Lloyd-Jones, *Life of Joy,* 205.

2. Lloyd-Jones, *Life of Joy,* 178–79.

Week 6: A Friend Like No Other

The epigraph is taken from J. I. Packer, *Knowing God* (Downers Grove, IL: Inter-Varsity, 1973), 35.

1. A. W. Tozer, *The Pursuit of God* (Harrisburg, PA: Christian Publications, 1948), 19.

Week 7: Something Better Is Coming

The epigraph is taken from J. I. Packer, *Knowing God* (Downers Grove, IL: Inter-Varsity, 1973), 207–8.

1. Martyn Lloyd-Jones, *The Life of Peace: An Exposition of Philippians 3 and 4* (London: Hodder and Stoughton, 1990), 127.
2. *The Beloved Works of C. S. Lewis: Surprised by Joy, Reflections on the Psalms, The Four Loves, The Business of Heaven* (New York: Inspirational, 1998), 297.
3. Lloyd-Jones, *Life of Peace*, 111.
4. Lloyd-Jones, *Life of Peace*, 99–100.
5. John Owen, *Overcoming Sin and Temptation*, ed. Kelly M. Kapic and Justin Taylor (Wheaton, IL: Crossway, 2006), 332.
6. Richard Baxter, *Practical Works* (Morgan, PA: Soli Deo Gloria, 1990, 2:884–85), quoted in Richard Rushing, ed., *Voices from the Past: Puritan Devotional Readings* (Edinburgh, Scotland: Banner of Truth, 2009), 138.
7. C. S. Lewis, *Mere Christianity* (New York: Macmillan, 1952), 118.

Week 8: A Heart at Peace

The epigraph is taken from Timothy Keller, *Prayer: Experiencing Awe and Intimacy with God* (New York: Dutton, 2014), 231.

1. Martyn Lloyd-Jones, *The Life of Peace: An Exposition of Philippians 3 and 4* (London: Hodder and Stoughton, 1990), 164.
2. J. B. Lightfoot, *St. Paul's Epistle to the Philippians* (Peabody, MA: Hendrickson, 1995), 161.
3. L. H. Marshall, *The Challenge of New Testament Ethics* (New York: Macmillan, 1966), 305–8.
4. Ralph P. Martin, *The Epistle of Paul to the Philippians: An Introduction and Commentary*, 2nd ed., The Tyndale New Testament Commentaries, vol. 11 (Grand Rapids, MI: Eerdmans, 1987), 172.

Week 9: Upside-Down Living
The epigraph is taken from Erik Raymond, *Chasing Contentment: Trusting God in a Discontented Age* (Wheaton, IL: Crossway, 2017), 25.

1. Martyn Lloyd-Jones, *Spiritual Depression: Its Causes and Its Cures* (Grand Rapids, MI: Eerdmans, 1965), 290.